MIGRAINE

ANSWERS TO

MIGRAINE

DR CLIFFORD ROSE
and
DR PAUL DAVIES

ILLUSTRATED BY ANDREA NORTON

An OPTIMA book

First published in 1987 by
Macdonald Optima, a division of
Macdonald & Co. (Publishers) Ltd

A BPCC PLC company

British Library Cataloguing in Publication Data

Rose, Clifford
    Migraine.——(Healthlines).
    1. Migraine
    I. title   II. Davies, Paul   III. Series
    616.8'57   RC392

    ISBN 0-356-12437-1

Macdonald & Co. (Publishers) Ltd
3rd Floor
Greater London House
Hampstead Road
London NW1 7QX

Typeset by Leaper & Gard Ltd, Bristol
Printed and bound in Great Britain by
The Guernsey Press Co. Ltd., Guernsey, Channel Islands.

CONTENTS

1.
WHAT IS MIGRAINE?

Migraine is the name given to a particular pattern of recurring physical symptoms of which the most distressing is usually headache. These symptoms vary in their nature and in the severity and frequency in different sufferers. In most cases, it is very easy to decide if someone has migraine but occasionally there is uncertainty because the diagnosis is made purely on the symptoms and, despite the ever-increasing complexity of tests available in medicine today, there is still no test for migraine. It is, of course, essential that the correct diagnosis is made, otherwise there can be no rational treatment.

Most of the symptoms of migraine are non-specific, that is, they also occur in other conditions. Headache occurs in nearly 50 different medical disorders, some of which are serious but the vast majority are not. All headache sufferers wonder at some time whether they have a brain tumour; this is almost invariably not the case, and with increasing knowledge of headache it is now possible to decide whether the headache is due to migraine, tension headache or some other condition.

In numerical terms, two disorders account for most headaches — muscle contraction (tension) headache and migraine. A third type, cluster headache, will also be described (see page 24), as this is often confused with migraine. Any sufferer who is uncertain about the cause of headaches should consult their general practitioner.

The symptoms of migraine have been recognised for

over 2,000 years and many famous people have suffered from it — Charles Darwin, Frederic Chopin, Virginia Woolf and David Frost to name but a few. However, it was less than 100 years ago that the first good account of migraine appeared and only in the last 50 years have we had some clues as to its nature and developed effective treatments. Despite a great deal of research, which continues today, the basic cause is still unclear. Ignorance produces speculation, anecdotes and old wives' tales to bewilder the sufferer looking for an effective solution to this distressing condition. However, once the correct diagnosis is made there is much that can be done to help; with self-help, or self-help combined with medication, most migraine sufferers can reduce their attack frequency and severity by at least half, and it is not uncommon for the attacks to be almost comply eliminated.

Many famous people have suffered from it --- Charles Darwin Frederic Chopin, Virginia Wolff and David Frost to name but a few.

The word migraine comes from the Greek term for a one-sided headache (*hemi-crain-ia*), but migraine does not have to be one-sided nor are all one-sided headaches due to migraine. Migraine is *never* just a headache since it *always* includes other symptoms which can be very varied, both in their nature and their severity. The headache can be extremely painful, suggesting to the sufferer that some serious damage is being done. Neurological symptoms may occur which are often alarming and some sufferers believe they are having a stroke. Sickness is very common and can sometimes be the worst feature of the attack. Occasionally, even headache does not occur and this may produce uncertainty as to the nature of the illness. We will outline the different symptoms that are seen in migraine, but it must be remembered that, as there are so many different varieties of symptoms, they will not all occur during a single attack.

THE PHYSICAL SYMPTOMS OF MIGRAINE

Headache

This is usually the worst part of the migraine attack. It may start anywhere on the head but is one-sided in nearly 70 per cent of cases. It is not severe from the moment of onset, the pain building up slowly over minutes or hours until it does become severe. Pain is always subjective and difficult to quantify but many people are generally unable to carry on their daily activities and are invariably forced to rest. The pain may have a throbbing quality which is in time with the pulse. Head movements, straining or even walking can worsen the pain and most people find it beneficial to lie down, although some prefer to sit upright. The duration of the headache is usually within the range of a few hours to three days.

Some people find relief by pressure on the head, e.g. tying a piece of cloth around the head, or by placing hot or cold packs over the area of pain. The site of the headache may change in different attacks or sometimes within the same attack, but it is not uncommon for people to experience the headache in the same place each time. The headache can start at any time of the day, although commonly on wakening. It seldom wakes people up during the night, which is a feature more typical of cluster headache (see page 24).

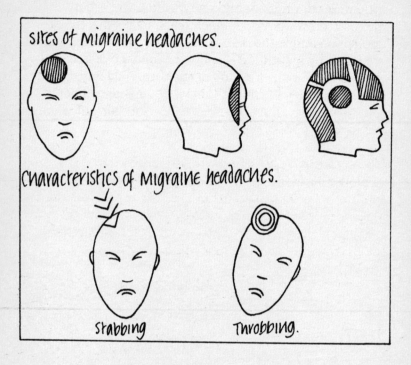

sites of migraine headaches.

characteristics of migraine headaches.

stabbing   Throbbing.

Migraine sufferers may also experience what are called ice-pick headaches — brief, sharp, piercing, one-sided headaches, not always associated with the migraine attack. These may occur several times a day and their cause is unknown.

Sickness

This is a very common complaint, about 95 per cent of migraine attacks being associated with nausea. Nausea may be felt at the onset of the attack or may occur as the headache reaches its peak, and the severity varies; some people experience profuse vomiting, more distressing than the headache itself, while others may just feel unlike eating. Those who are sick may find this relieves the headache for a while and in such cases they may deliberately induce vomiting to ease the headache. Where vomiting is severe it may not be possible to keep even a little water down, and mild dehydration can occur. Sickness prevents the stomach doing its normal job of absorption and is the reason why many painkillers which are taken by mouth are found to be ineffective in easing the headache, since they do not get into the body. Some people find they vomit the tablets up unchanged hours after they have taken them, and this is important when treatment is considered.

Photophobia and phonophobia

Photophobia is the dislike of light — a very common symptom during a migraine attack. Most sufferers prefer to close the curtains and rest during this time.

Phonophobia is the dislike of sound, and is another common symptom during the migraine attack.

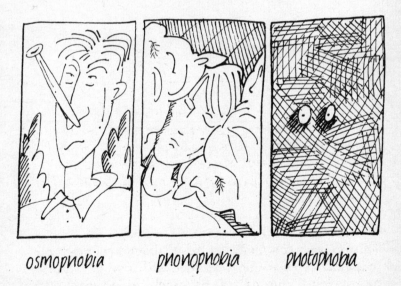

osmophobia   phonophobia   photophobia

Osmophobia

The dislike of smells such as cooking smells or perfume occurs in many sufferers during migraine attacks.

During a migraine attack it should now be apparent that the sufferer is over-sensitive to many types of stimuli, probably reflecting the irritability of the brain.

Change in temperature sensation
Some people feel hot or cold, shiver or sweat during the attack.

Change in bowel habit
Diarrhoea is not infrequent during a migraine attack and reflects the change in the autonomic nervous system (that part of the nervous system that controls automatic bodily functions) at this time. Its occurrence does make the use of suppositories as a means of administering drugs difficult or impossible.

Change in urinary frequency
The passing of large quantities of dilute urine (polyuria) is a recognised but rare symptom of the migraine attack.

Change in blood vessels
Rarely there may be bruising of the skin, particularly around the eyes, as part of the migraine attack.

The above symptoms are found in both the two main types of migraine — common migraine and classical migraine (see pages 17 to 20) — in the latter the neurological symptoms almost invariably occur before the start of the headache.

THE NEUROLOGICAL SYMPTOMS OF MIGRAINE

These are part of the migraine attack, usually last for about half an hour (a range of 10-60 minutes) before the headache begins and are collectively termed the aura of migraine. On the first occasion they can be alarming since some people feel that something is seriously wrong, e.g. they think they are having a stroke. While these symptoms *are* due to change within the brain, they do *not* cause any permanent brain damage and the disability is only temporary. The areas of the brain most commonly affected are those concerned with eyesight, the limbs and speech.

These neurological symptoms only occur in what is known as classical migraine. They last for about half an hour and, as they disappear, the headache and sickness begin, although there may be a short gap (up to 15 minutes) between the end of the aura and the onset of the headache.

If the headache and sickness commence without any of these neurological symptoms occurring first, the attack is called common migraine. Less commonly, a headache does not follow the neurological symptoms, in which case the attack is called a migraine equivalent (see page 20).

Visual symptoms

The visual symptoms during the migraine attack take different forms, but can be very dramatic. At one end of the scale there is blurred vision which is quite common, but the most characteristic neurological symptom of migraine is the spreading scintillating scotoma (see page 15). This starts as a small blind area (scotoma), usually in the centre of the field of view, which gradually expands affecting more and more of the half-field of vision. The edge of this blind spot is surrounded by shimmering (scintillating) lights which may take 20 to 30 minutes to cross the whole field of view (see page 15). The spreading scintillating scotoma is characteristic of migraine and occurs in no other condition.

Whilst the loss of vision is a negative phenomenon, the scintillation (shimmering lights) is positive. The visual fields may be broken up and interrupted by shiny lines or arranged like constellations. This phenomenon is known as a fortification spectrum (see page 15) because it resembles a castellated fort — hence the medical term teichopsia (from *teichos* which is Greek for a wall). There may also be flashing sparks or stars (photopsia), zig-zag patterns or Catherine wheels. These hallucinations can be very vivid and have even been the subject for saintly visions and, more recently, art competitions.

The loss of vision (negative phenomenon) may occur in a roughly semi-circular area or there can be multiple blind spots. Sometimes loss of half of a visual field occurs so that, for example, objects on the left side can be seen, the right side being blacked out. The reason for this loss of half the field of view is that the brain is made up of two hemispheres and each hemisphere sees only half of the field of view. The right hemisphere sees (processes visual information) from the left half of the field of view and vice-versa, so that when one half of the brain is affected during a migraine attack there is loss of half of the opposite visual field. If both hemispheres are affected at the same time there can be tunnel vision and even complete loss of vision.

While there may be either positive or negative features during the visual aura (the beginning of the attack), it is more common for both types to occur together. Both result from temporary disturbances of the covering part (cortex) of the back part of the brain that deals with vision (occipital lobes). Less common disturbances of vision include changes in the perception of objects, where the size and shape is altered, or they appear too big or too far away or angled, or their colours faded. These symptoms occur when those areas of the brain responsible for spatial orientation (the parietal lobes) are involved. The perception of one's own body image may even be affected so that patients complain that they feel taller or smaller than normal. It is because of this that it was thought that Lewis Carroll, a migraine sufferer, was drawing on his own experience of such sensations when he wrote *Alice in Wonderland*, but there is some doubt about this as he is said to have developed his migraine after he wrote the book.

Limbs

Just as positive and negative features can occur with visual symptoms, so they also occur in the limbs, although the positive ones tend to predominate. For example, pins

SCINTILLATING
SCOTOMA.

SHIMMERING
LIGHTS.

FORTIFICATION
SPECTRUM.

and needles can occur, generally on one side of the body, starting in the hand and spreading up the arm. They are transient, lasting only a few minutes. The face and tongue can also be affected. Much less commonly there is weakness of a limb or of one side of the body which can rarely become completely paralysed for a short period.

Speech

Speech may be affected in a migraine attack. Usually before the headache starts there may be a slurring of words or even difficulty in finding the correct words and putting them into a coherent sentence. In most people the speech centre is in the left cerebral hemisphere and so marked speech difficulties can arise when the other neurological symptoms (loss of vision or pins and needles) affect the right side of the body.

Other neurological symptoms

While visual symptoms are the most common of the neurological symptoms seen in migraine, a combination of visual, limb and speech symptoms may occur. These symptoms may always start on the same side of the body, but the reason for this is unknown and it should certainly not be a cause for concern about any serious underlying condition. Which of these neurological symptoms occur depends on what part of the brain is affected by the migraine process, some parts being more commonly affected than others. Alterations in consciousness, double vision, distorted perception of sound and dizziness are all common. Migraine sufferers are often reluctant to talk about the more bizarre of these neurological symptoms for fear of being ridiculed, but there is always a clear neurological explanation.

There is another group of symptoms which are almost certainly neurological in origin, which are more vague, last longer than the aura, and occur up to 24 hours before the attack starts. These 'premonitory' symptoms are sensations which are not really appropriate for that particular time and consist of mood changes, with feelings of excessive energy, some people feeling they could do anything on these days. Others may feel depressed or lethargic, with feelings of hunger, thirst or just a vague sensation that something is about to happen. Some people feel particularly aware of colour, sound or smells. These symptoms generally occur the day before the attack proper and probably result from a chemical imbalance within important control centres in the lower part of the brain (the hypothalamus). These premonitory or warning symptoms, although undoubtedly of neurological origin, are not deciding factors as to whether the attacks are common or classical migraine since they are not sufficiently localised, i.e. focal.

None of these symptoms of migraine, apart from the scintillating scotoma, are specific for migraine, although the more features that are present the more certain the diagnosis of migraine. If only a few features are present, it may be difficult to be sure that we are dealing with migraine and since the symptoms are so varied, it is almost impossible to produce a definition which includes all attacks of migraine. What is essential for the diagnosis of migraine is that there should be a recurrent headache with complete freedom from symptoms between attacks. An individual patient may suffer from one type of migraine at different times and some patients may also suffer from muscle contraction (tension) headache. However, the diagnostic borders of each condition, particularly common migraine and tension headache, are not always clearly demarcated.

THE VARIETIES OF MIGRAINE

Common migraine

As implied, this is by far the most common variety of migraine. The headache is associated with nausea and there may be photophobia and phonophobia. The headache is less often unilateral (one-sided) than with classical migraine (described below) and it is more likely

17

to be triggered by events, circumstances, sensory stimuli or food (collectively called trigger factors). The popular terms 'dietary', 'weekend', 'menstrual' and 'footballers' migraine are all synonymous with common migraine. Common migraine accounts for more misery and suffering than all the other types of migraine put together as at least two-thirds of all migraine attacks are of this variety.

Most common migraine attacks last for a day or less and it is rare for them to continue for more than three days. The day prior to the migraine attack there may be warning symptoms which people may come to recognise as the beginning of a migraine attack. The headache often begins when the patient first wakes up in the morning; at first it is usually mild and can be on one side of the head or on both sides. During the course of a single attack the pain may change from one side to the other or move around on the same side or change from a one-sided to an 'all over' (generalised) headache. As the day progresses the headache becomes more severe and nausea develops. Similarly, photophobia and phonophobia become prominent and the patient is confined to bed, preferably in a darkened room. As vomiting occurs in about 40 per cent of attacks, a bowl should be near to hand. Because vomiting can produce a marked reduction in the severity of the headache, some sufferers deliberately make themselves sick. The sufferer looks unwell, the face may be pale and cold while the scalp and forehead are hot and may be flushed on the side of the headache.

After a variable time the pain and sickness subside, the patient feels washed out and full recovery may not occur until many hours or days later. However, some people recover remarkably quickly, and may even feel exhilarated; others feel depressed at the end of the attack.

While this describes the common migraine attack, the severity and combination of symptoms is variable and rarely are attacks exactly the same.

Classical migraine
Classical migraine is like common migraine but the

attacks are preceded by neurological symptoms (the aura). Many people experience both common and classical migraine during their lifetime, sometimes beginning wih classical migraine in youth and developing common migraine in later life. Classical migraine attacks are generally less frequent than those of common migraine and each attack tends to be of shorter duration.

Many varieties of classical migraine exist. Some that are very uncommon may cause diagnostic difficulties and sufferers should consult their general practitioners. The following sub-types of classical migraine are perhaps the most important:

- Vertebro-basilar migraine
- Hemiplegic migraine
- Ophthalmoplegic migraine
- Retinal migraine

Vertebro-basilar migraine (basilar artery migraine) is a type of classical migraine that affects about one-tenth of migraine sufferers. It is particularly common among young women and adolescent girls. The neurological symptoms include unsteadiness, confusion, dizziness, slurred speech, ringing in the ears, numbness around the mouth and the tongue and one-sided or bilateral loss of vision. In some patients there is impairment or even loss of consciousness. These symptoms generally last 30 to 45 minutes and commonly persist into the headache phase and may even worsen during this time. The name comes from the basilar artery which supplies blood to those structures in the brain, the dysfunction of which produces these symptoms.

Hemiplegic migraine is a rare type of classical migraine where there is weakness of one side of the body which occurs during the headache phase and may be prolonged. The condition may run in families.

Ophthalmoplegic migraine again is a rare form of migraine and occurs particularly in young children, producing double vision. The neurological problems relate to the control of eye movement and, since these defects become apparent after the onset of headache, it is not typical of classical migraine. With recurrent attacks the defects may persist and require medical investigation.

Retinal migraine is a very rare form of migraine and its existence has even been challenged. The neurological symptoms preceding the attack indicate that the disturbance is in the retina — the light-sensitive area at the back of the eye. The visual symptoms clearly occur in only one eye.

Migraine equivalents

These are commoner than previously thought. In classical migraine the headache is preceded by a disturbance of brain function, but if this dysfunction is *not* followed by a headache then the attack is termed a migraine equivalent. The visual symptoms typical of classical migraine may occur in isolation, particularly in older patients, with no subsequent headache. When there is a history of previous classical migraine the diagnosis is easier to make. Migraine equivalents are quite common in young children, who commonly suffer from what is termed abdominal migraine (see below). Migraine equivalents can often be confused with other conditions and it is not uncommon for patients to have undergone extensive investigations before the real diagnosis becomes apparent.

Migraine in children

Migraine is frequent in children and is usually of the common variety. Some, however, suffer from what is known as abdominal migraine, which applies to certain symptoms thought to be related to migraine, e.g. recurrent attacks of prolonged and often severe stomach pain typically associated with pallor of the face, loss of appetite, nausea or vomiting. Some children go on to have more typical migraine in later life. Other conditions less clearly associated with typical migraine are recurrent (cyclical) vomiting, 'growing pains' and bilious attacks.

2.
HEADACHES OTHER THAN MIGRAINE

In this chapter we shall look at a number of other types of headache, many of which are frequently confused with migraine.

The two types of headache that are perhaps most frequently confused with migraine are muscle-contraction (tension) headache and cluster headache. The causes, mechanisms and treatments of these two types of headache are different from migraine and so must be differentiated. This is not always easy and so we will describe the symptoms of each.

MUSCLE-CONTRACTION (TENSION) HEADACHE

Tension headache is the most common type of headache. Many people think the word 'tension' implies emotional tension and that this then produces headache. However, tension in this context really means muscle tension and perhaps the term muscle-contraction headache is a better one. Unlike migraine, tension headache generally has no other symptom besides the headache. Other symptoms may occur but are subsequent to the cause of tension headache or else result from the headache. It is therefore referred to as a primary headache.

MUSCLE CONTRACTION (TENSION) HEADACHE

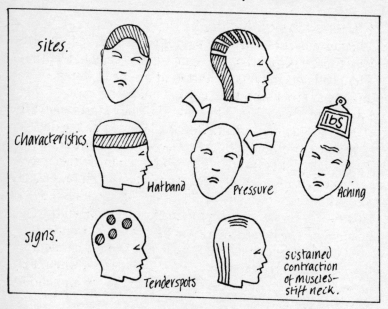

sites.

characteristics. — Hatband — Pressure — Aching

signs. — Tenderspots — sustained contraction of muscles—stiff neck.

The headache

The pain of tension headache is nearly always on both sides of the head at the same time, e.g. across the forehead, temples, top or back of the head, and in the neck, with the pain sometimes extending towards the shoulders. The pain is rarely severe; that is, rarely severe enough to force the sufferer home from work. People describe the pain as a pressure, tightness, constriction, ache, vice-like and like wearing a tight hat or helmet. The pain seems to be due to the muscles in the neck or scalp contracting in certain areas (tender spots) rather than throughout the muscles. Two types of tension headache may occur.

Acute tension headache

This headache starts when there is stress, and goes away on relaxation. It is extremely common — most people have experienced it. The cause is usually obvious and massaging the muscles in the neck or rubbing the head usually gives some relief from the pain.

Chronic tension headache

This form occurs when the pain has been present for a long time, e.g. months. The cause is less easy to identify. The headache may have started at a time of worry, anxiety or stress and then carried on, perhaps intermittently at first. This pain typically starts soon after waking in the morning and tends to worsen as the day progresses. However, it never wakes the patient at night. Painkillers either have no effect on the pain or else may just numb it for a while. The chronic condition may easily result in a large consumption of painkillers which may not only be dangerous but can, paradoxically, worsen the headache. The headache varies in severity but may worsen when under stress; conversely, when occupied, the pain may be forgotten until further relaxation, when it is noticed again. Sufferers may find it is relieved on holiday or at weekends.

To demonstrate this form of headache, and that it is a result of altered muscle tension, if we press down on the head or gently exert traction on the neck this often produces temporary relief by altering the tension in the muscles. Neck movements may be reduced due to the muscle spasm. Feeling (palpation of) the neck muscles may reveal areas of the muscle that are knotted and very tender.

Other symptoms of tension headache

While tension headache typically has no other symptoms, anxiety and depression may be present and may produce their own symptoms. Anxiety symptoms include a rapid heart beat, intermittent dizziness, sweating and difficulty in relaxing; those of depression may be lethargy, poor sleeping, weight loss and difficulty in concentrating.

The treatment of tension headache is different from that of migraine. Depression may require antidepressant medication such as amitriptyline (Tryptizol), anxiety treatment may involve the intermittent use of tranquillisers such as diazepam (Valium) and symptomatic treatment may include neck massage, physiotherapy or relaxation techniques.

CLUSTER HEADACHE

Sometimes called migrainous neuralgia, this condition is often confused with migraine but it is quite distinct. As the name implies, a series of headaches occur in clusters lasting 6-12 weeks and may recur every year, sometimes with quite remarkable timing. During the cluster-period characteristic symptoms occur daily or even several times a day. Often the sufferer is woken up in the early hours of the morning (1-3 am) with a severe one-sided headache, usually centred around the eye.

During this cluster-period the headache is always on the same side of the head. The pain is very severe, often excruciating, and lasts half to two hours, occasionally a bit longer. It comes on quite quickly, unlike migraine which slowly builds up. The sufferer prefers to pace about the room, rather than lie still as in a migraine attack. Besides the severe pain there are other typical features which occur on the same side of the head as the pain. These include:

- Red watery eye
- Stuffiness of or runny nostril
- Drooping of the eyelid

Unlike migraine, cluster headache is much more common in men, especially those who are usually heavy smokers. The trigger factors (see pages 42 and 62) associated with migraine are not seen in cluster headache, apart from alcohol, which can set off an attack in the cluster period.

Sometimes these headaches do not show a clustering pattern but just continue, maybe two or three times a week, for long periods. This is termed chronic cluster

CLUSTER HEADACHE

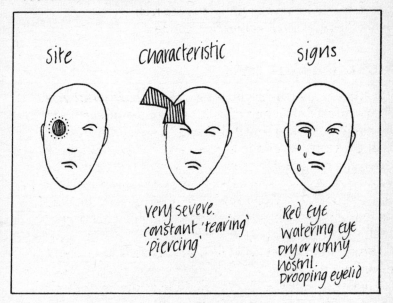

Site   Characteristic   signs.

very severe.
constant 'tearing'
'piercing'

Red eye,
watering eye
Dry or runny
nostril.
Drooping eyelid

headache. Rarely, features of cluster headache and migraine are seen in the same patient in the condition termed cluster migraine.

The treatment for cluster headache is often very successful but is different from that for migraine. The attacks may be prevented by the use of lithium but they also respond to steroids, oxygen and ergotamine.

There are at least 30,000 sufferers from cluster headache in Britain and perhaps a lot more who have not been diagnosed. If you feel you have this condition you should seek medical advice because, although it causes no damage (the severe pain suggests something terrible is happening), the specific treatment is only available on prescription.

In the following sections, we will discuss the investigation of headache and briefly describe those rarer headache conditions which have an underlying identifiable cause.

SECONDARY HEADACHES

These headaches have a clearer cause than primary headaches, in that they are secondary to an identifiable cause. There is no perfect classification of headache, and sometimes no identifiable underlying cause can be found. However, some of the more common ones will be discussed.

Neuralgias

The term neuralgia, often used vaguely, is meant for specific conditions, the commonest of which are trigeminal neuralgia and post-herpetic neuralgia.

Trigeminal neuralgia occurs over the age of 40 with a lightning or shooting pain in the region of the cheek, jaw or forehead, lasting from a few seconds up to half a minute. The severe pain affects one side of the head only, and is triggered by touch, cold, wind, chewing or loud noise. The discomfort is such that it is often difficult to wash on that side of the face or to chew. There is seldom any underlying cause, but treatment with a drug called carbamazepine (Tegretol) is very effective.

Post-herpetic neuralgia or shingles is caused by the herpes zoster virus (which can also cause chickenpox) infecting the nerves in the face. The nerve most commonly affected is on one side of the forehead. Shingles consists of blisters on the skin and pain occurs before and after the eruption of this rash. When persistent, it can be severe and treatment is sometimes difficult.

Atypical facial pain

This pain is felt in the cheek, teeth or gums and is continuous and boring in quality. The pain may date from minor dental treatment or an injury to the face. The basic cause is unknown but it may be associated with depression. Migraine and cluster headache can both cause pain in this area and those with gum and tooth pain due to these conditions may end up having some teeth out to see if it makes any difference.

Pain due to problems with the eyes and ears

Disorders of the eye (e.g. glaucoma) may produce pain in the eye, though it is unusual for eye problems to cause pain in the head. Imbalance of the muscles supplying the eyes, as in squints or lens problems that require glasses may contribute to tension headache but do not cause migraine.

Ear problems are common in children and may be linked with some degree of deafness; looking at the ear drum will give the answer in most cases.

Just as alcohol can cause a headache, so too can monosodium glutamate (Chinese-restaurant syndrome), nitrites and nitrates (hot-dog headache).

Chinese-restaurant syndrome

Chinese meals may contain a lot of monosodium glutamate (a substance that enhances flavouring). Some people find that within half an hour of starting a Chinese meal (particularly after soup) they develop a headache

Chinese restaurant syndrome.

which is usually in the forehead and temples. Besides the headache they may experience pressure or tightness over the face and chest.

Hot-dog headache
Nitrites are used in curing meat to give it a uniform colour. These substances are also vaso-dilators (dilate the blood vessels), so that some people find that soon after eating these meats they develop flushing of the face and a headache. The hot-dog is the classical example but other culprits include bacon, ham and salami.

Headache can be caused by drug withdrawal. The classical example of this sort of headache is alcohol withdrawal — the hangover. While the explanation of the hangover is not entirely clear it is probably a result of several different mechanisms. Some find that another drink helps the hangover, which implies that drug withdrawal is a possible mechanism.

Caffeine withdrawal
Tea and coffee addicts often find they have a headache if they have not had caffeine recently.

Ergotamine withdrawal
This is often a difficult problem to deal with. Ergotamine is a strong drug which can be very useful in getting rid of some migraine attacks. However, it is also addictive and so should only be used very occasionally (once every 6-8 weeks). If it is used more frequently, as is often the case, then frequent migraine may turn into a frequent ergotamine withdrawal condition which itself gives headache as well as nausea and general malaise — symptoms similar to migraine and which respond very well when ergotamine is taken.

Tea and coffee addicts often find they have a headache if they have not had caffeine recently.

Analgesic withdrawal

Regular, frequent analgesic consumption can also produce a withdrawal headache.

There are several other common triggers of headache.

Ice-cream headache

If a very cold substance such as ice cream or an ice-cold drink is swallowed or held in the mouth the intense cooling causes a pain which is felt in the head. This ice-cream headache is more common in those susceptible to migraine. The headache is usually in the frontal region but in some migrainous patients it is felt in the habitual site of the migraine headache. Similar headaches may result from diving into cold water.

Cough headache

This is a rare form of headache where coughing brings on

ice cream headache.

a headache. There may be no identifiable cause but investigations are usually performed. If none is found, the headache may go after a variable period of time.

Exertional headache
Like the cough headache, exertion may bring on a headache which has no obvious cause although, again, investigations are usually done.

High blood pressure
There is very little correlation between blood pressure and headache. Only when the blood pressure is dangerously raised is headache a real feature. Whilst high blood pressure may aggravate migraine and should be treated, the commonest cause of headache in hypertension is anxiety.

Benign orgasmic cephalalgia
This is a well-recognised headache that occurs only during sexual intercourse and at the time around orgasm. It is a

severe pain which may last from a few minutes to several hours. It is more common in men and has no serious cause. There is an association with migraine and treatment along the lines used in migraine may be helpful.

3.
THE INVESTIGATION OF HEADACHE

To reach any diagnosis, the approach usually used by doctors is as follows:

- To take a history of the symptoms.
- To examine the patient for any abnormality.
- Take tests if necessary.
- Try a specific form of therapy.

In migraine there are no abnormalities to find on examining the patient and there are no reliable tests to confirm the diagnosis. That leaves us with taking a history of symptoms and trying a specific form of therapy. A few people with rare types of migraine may have undergone several investigations, so a range of tests that are used in the investigation of headache today will be described. Most of these tests look at the structure and composition of the skull and its contents rather than the function of the nervous tissue, but most headaches originate from a dysfunction of the nerves or blood vessels in the head.

There are no known structural abnormalities in tension headache, migraine or cluster headache, which are termed primary headaches. The much smaller group of headaches which may arise from structural abnormalities, or which at least have some recognisable pathological process causing them, are termed secondary headaches. It is in the investigation of these secondary headaches that powerful tools are available, as described below. It is likely that only when we understand the biochemical mechanisms of migraine will any such specific tests become available.

TESTS FOR MIGRAINE

There are three tests that are sometimes used when diagnosing migraine:

- Cytotoxic test
- Skin tests
- Radio-absorbant test

The cytotoxic test

This test is based on a simple idea. Foods are often blamed as the cause of migraine and it appears that alcohol, chocolate, cheese and citrus fruit can trigger migraine in some people, although we do not know how

Alcohol, chocolate, cheese and citrus fruit can trigger migraine in some people.

these foods set off the attack. If a blood sample is taken from a migraine sufferer and small amounts are added to extracts of various foods, then some of the blood cells may be damaged by the food extract. This damage can be seen through a microscope and so, on testing against a large number of food extracts, a profile of so-called food allergies can be determined.

This is the principle of the test; it is attractive, but it is of no proven use in the management of migraine. The results of the test apparently depend very much on the laboratory doing the tests (not done in the National Health Service). There are reports in the medical literature looking at the validity and reproducibility of this test and the conclusions were that it was unreliable. It is a harmless test but is relatively expensive. However, if a food substance is going to produce migraine it should do so within 24 hours of consumption and the cause should usually be obvious.

Skin tests

This is again an attractive idea. Like the cytotoxic test, various food extracts are produced but this time they are injected into the skin. After a while any reaction produced in the skin is noted and it is then inferred that that food extract can cause migraine in that patient. There is a clearer association between this test and allergic conditions such as asthma, where this sort of test is useful. However, migraine is *not* an allergic condition and there is no correlation between the skin test and the cause of migraine.

Radio-absorbant (RAST) test

The radio-absorbant test simply measures antibodies in the blood to certain foods. There is no correlation between antibodies and migraine and this test is of no use in predicting the cause of migraine.

There is only one way of finding out what triggers migraine and that is by looking for patterns of association, as discussed in the next chapter.

However, certain tests can be used to diagnose other forms of headache, and we will now go on to look at some of these tests.

BLOOD TEST

There is only one condition where blood tests really help the diagnosis of a headache condition and this is temporal arteritis. This disease occurs only in those over the age of 55 and is due to an inflammation of the arteries in the scalp. Three consequences of this are:

- Headache, due to the swollen painful artery.
- Visual symptoms, when the artery supplying blood to the eye is involved in the inflammation — there is less blood supply to the eye, with subsequent loss of vision, and permanent blindness can result.
- Feelings of general malaise due to the effects of generalised inflammation.

The blood test done in this condition is the erythrocyte sedimentation rate (ESR), where a column of blood is held in a glass tube and the rate at which the red cells (erythrocytes) fall to the bottom (sedimentation) is measured and is expressed in millimetres per hour. The ESR in temporal arteritis is very high. Usually a small piece of artery is biopsied (taken out and examined) so that specific changes can be seen under the microscope. The treatment is with steroids which produce relief within hours.

X-RAY EXAMINATION

X-rays only show up dense structure like bone so that only those conditions producing bony abnormalities or shadows will be seen, for example:

- Teeth problems — may show an abscess.
- Neck problems — arthritis in the neck can cause headache.
- Sinus disease — chronic sinusitis causes thickening and sometimes fluid in the sinuses, which shows up on X-ray.
- Pituitary tumour — this is one of the few tumours which, because they erode bone, show up on a skull X-ray.

Unless one of these conditions is suspected, there is little place for routine skull X-rays in the investigation of headache.

PROBLEMS WITHIN THE SKULL

For possible problems within the skull, there are several investigations which can be done, one of the most important of which is a lumbar puncture.

Lumbar puncture
This allows a sample of cerebro-spinal fluid (CSF) to be removed for analysis. Many people have heard of this test, and done correctly it is virtually painless since local anaesthetic is administered at the bottom of the spine and a fine needle is introduced. The pressure of the cerebro-spinal fluid is measured and the fluid can be analysed. This test can reveal the following causes of headache:

Subarachnoid haemorrhage, where the headache is usually at the back of the head, severe and of sudden onset. Due to a burst blood vessel on the surface of the brain, it is a serious condition and requires an operation.

Meningitis, which is an inflammation of the surface of the brain due to germs such as bacteria and viruses. Besides the headache there is a fever, neck stiffness and an intense dislike of the light (photophobia).

DISEASES OF THE BRAIN ITSELF

Brain tissue itself is insensitive to pain, but headaches can be due to a distortion of the large arteries which supply the brain with blood, the large veins draining blood from the brain, and the covering of the brain itself (meninges), since these are all pain sensitive.

Disease of the brain tissue may cause:

- Loss of function, such as weakness or paralysis
- Change in personality
- Fits

If the cause of the headache is a growth (tumour) or some other space-occupying abnormality, then two other consequences may be:

- Raised pressure within the skull producing pain and eventually drowsiness and coma
- Blockage of the normal CSF pathways causing hydrocephalus — treated by an operation to insert a drain or shunt

Only when pain-sensitive structures within the skull are stimulated can a headache occur and headache is often not a prominent feature of brain tumours.

Electro-encephalogram (EEG)

Most people will have heard of the electro-cardiogram (ECG) which measures the electrical activity of the heart; from the wave pattern produced, abnormalities can be detected. So, too, the electrical activity of the brain may be recorded by placing small metal electrodes on the scalp and the activity measured by using an EEG.

There are certain normal patterns of electrical activity. When the eyes are closed, a normal (alpha) rhythm appears, which lessens when the eyes are opened. Fast rhythms may be seen when the patient is on tranquillisers and slower waves indicate malfunction or tumours within the brain.

The EEG, in general, does not reveal the specific abnormality causing the disturbance, its main use being in the study of epileptic conditions.

Brain scanning

There are three main types of scan which are in use today and can tell us a great deal about the structures within the skull:

Radioactive isotopes, where the patient is given an injection of a short-lasting radioactive isotope into an arm vein. It travels to the brain in the bloodstream and is distributed according to the blood flow and the type of tissue. The radioactivity is then measured using a special camera so that areas of stroke or tumour can be shown.

Computerised tomography (CT) scanning, which has revolutionised the investigation of serious headaches. By passing X-rays in various directions, and using a computer to process the images, a 3D picture of the brain is built up in great detail. Usually a contrast material is injected into a vein to aid definition of blood vessels and other vascular structures. Such scanners are very expensive and not available in all hospitals.

Magnetic resonance imaging (MRI) is one of the latest advances in the application of high technology to modern medicine. Without needing contrast and not involving X-rays, high definition of intra-cranial contents can be achieved. The principal is based on a strong magnetic field which vibrates molecules which in turn give off energy which can be detected. Again a 3D picture of the brain can be built up by computer.

Angiography

The blood vessels supplying blood to the brain can be shown by injecting a dye which blocks X-rays (in contrast to the soft tissues adjacent to the blood vessels). Called angiography, this test may involve admission into hospital as it is often performed under a general anaesthetic. A

39

catheter is introduced into the artery, either in the groin or in the neck, and several X-ray pictures are taken as the dye is injected. This investigation shows abnormal blood vessels, both arteries and veins.

Alternatively, a contrast dye can be injected into an arm vein and X-ray pictures taken once the dye reaches the artery. A computer is then used to image the arteries. This test is called digital subtraction angiography, and hospital admission is not always required.

4.
WHY DO WE GET MIGRAINE?

Whilst there are no abnormal findings in migraine, either on examination or on investigation, the symptoms are very real and result from biochemical changes which are poorly understood. The wide variety of symptoms and great diversity of trigger factors have made some doctors wonder whether migraine is a distinct disorder. Whilst it seems likely that there is a common mechanism to the production of migraine, the nature of this reaction or pathway is still controversial.

The vast number of sufferers and the great variation in frequency of attacks has posed the philosophical question as to whether migraine serves any purpose. It is not a disease in the usual meaning of the word since, while it causes much suffering, it produces no long-term physical or mental disability. Perhaps the only common finding amongst sufferers during an attack is the desire to withdraw from the world, to seek out a dark quiet stimulus-free environment where the most effective treatment of all, sleep, will bring about recovery. If migraine does serve any purpose it may be the removal of the sufferer from the triggers of migraine. In many sufferers this possible defence mechanism appears to be very over-active.

Although one day it may be possible to describe the processes of migraine in clear biochemical terms and explain how it can be triggered, we are still a long way from this goal. However, despite our ignorance of the fundamental cause of migraine, there is still a lot we can

41

do to help sufferers. An important aspect of treatment is for the sufferer to be aware of the nature of migraine, why it might occur, and what can be done to prevent it. In this chapter we shall consider why some people get migraine, under what circumstances it occurs and how the various symptoms are produced.

The cause of migraine is multifactorial, depending both on the genetic make-up of the individual, i.e. inherent personality traits, as well as factors in the environment. The importance of each will vary in different people but both aspects need to be considered.

WHO GETS MIGRAINE?

Migraine is a very common condition. Estimates vary, but probably up to 10 per cent of men and 20 per cent of women suffer from migraine at some time in their lives. From studying whole communities we know that many people suffer from migraine without realising what it is, and many sufferers have never seen their doctor about it. If we look at different populations within Britain, e.g. prisons, schools, particular areas of the country, there is no great variation in this frequency. Similarly, studies in Europe and elsewhere in the world support these figures. In Africa, migraine is much less frequently seen, except in the larger cities. Migraine is common in children but boys are more likely to be affected than girls. In any individual, migraine is unpredictable in frequency, but in migraine sufferers as a whole it improves with age. Comparatively few old people are troubled with migraine.

Inheritance
Studies of families with migraine have shown that migraine can be a strongly inherited condition — about 70 per cent of sufferers have a close family member with the condition. The study of identical twins, particlarly when they are brought up apart from one another, is a powerful method of looking for inherited factors in any disease. These studies again show that inheritance is an important

factor, although there is no clear method of inheritance. If the father is affected, then there is an early age of onset in his children.

When the type of migraine and the different trigger factors are studied within a family there are usually no close correlations, except for hemiplegic migraine (see page 19), which can affect most of the family, starting at a similar age as well as having common trigger factors.

Age of onset
Migraine may start for the first time at almost any age but it is unusual to start after the age of 50. Ninety per cent of sufferers have had their first attack before the age of 40, and it is common in children and young adults.

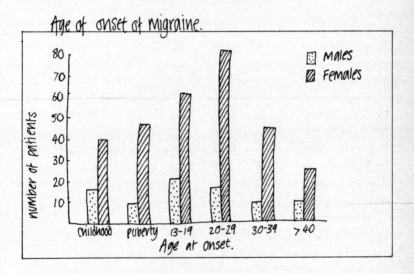

Age of onset of migraine.

The migrainous personality
There has been debate over the type of personality that is associated with migraine. The view that migraine affects mainly intelligent and successful people has been disproven; what is true is that these are the sort of people more likely to seek medical advice. In fact migraine is evenly distributed throughout the social strata.

Whilst it is generally considered that many migraine sufferers are perfectionist, ambitious, compulsive and rigid, many are anxious, hyperactive and have difficulty in relaxing. In 1960 a study was made of the personality profile of 500 migraine sufferers from all walks of life, and revealed that about a quarter showed obsessional behaviour (meticulous, double-checking their actions) whilst a similar number admitted that they had difficulty relaxing, were over-active and restless. Over 10 per cent were anxious, with difficulty in sleeping, while less than 50 per cent considered that they were relaxed and without ambitious or obsessional character traits. Certainly many people with frequent migraine show signs of anxiety and depression, but it is difficult to know whether depression is the cause or the result of frequent migraine.

Whilst genetic make-up cannot be changed, personality is adaptable and offers one gateway for treatment in some severely affected sufferers.

THE INFLUENCE OF TRIGGER FACTORS

Migraine is a recurring condition in which the periods between attacks are without any symptoms. Attacks may be set off in a variety of ways by what are collectively termed trigger factors. Some lists of possible trigger factors include an enormous, bewildering, variety which cover most aspects of human life. It is hard to believe that all these factors are important, let alone consider ways of avoiding them. However, it is difficult to be certain as to what is and what is not a trigger factor, particularly as there are no specific tests. There are two ways to help answer this question:

- People's perceptions as to what cause attacks are often circumstantial and biased by what they have been told; for example, chocolate is often quoted as being a trigger factor for migraine but on further questioning many people are unsure. If sufferers suspect some food or other, they will avoid it, and few will accept the challenge of eating that food to see if the migraine was more than merely a chance occurrence.

- The only way to prove the link scientifically is to carry out a double-blind placebo-controlled trial. This means getting together a group of sufferers who think a certain food brings on their migraine and giving them either the food or a dummy (the placebo) which looks and tastes like the real thing but is inactive. After this experiment those who develop migraine can be compared with what they were really given. This type of study has not often been done, so most evidence remains circumstantial.

Most attacks in fact result from a combination of factors, and it is uncommon for just one factor to set off a migraine attack. Trigger factors may be environmental, and this can be important in preventing migraine attacks. These environmental factors can be divided into two categories:

- Internal — cyclical events like sleep or menstruation, which are within us.
- External — the circumstances or situations found during daily life, including the various sensory and other stimuli to which we are constantly exposed.

Internal environment
Many biological events in man and nature follow a cyclical pattern, e.g. sleep, menstruation, and cyclical changes in mood, which are part of recurrent physiological cycles. Cluster headache can be closely linked to the seasons and to our own biological clock, and migraine similarly can be locked into various internal cyclical events.

Menstruation and migraine attacks are often closely related though some women have an attack at the time of ovulation. Usually, there is not an exact relationship. One

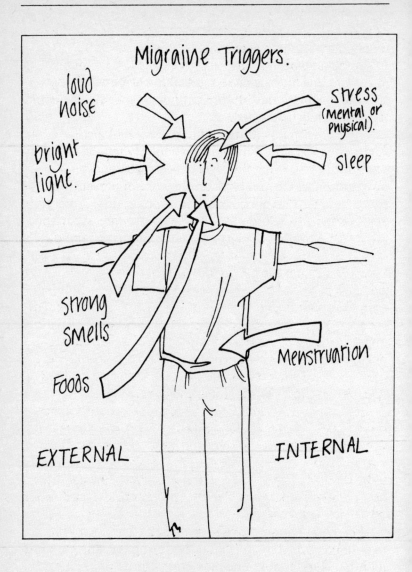

month the attack may occur on the few pre-menstrual days, the next it may occur during or just after menstruation. In a few women the attacks occur at exactly the same time of the month each month, a variety of common migraine termed menstrual migraine.

Migraine may start at the time of a woman's first period and stop at the time of the menopause.

Occasionally migraine can get worse at the time of the menopause and can even start at this time.

There have been many studies of this hormonal form of migraine, but there is no recognisable hormonal change specific for migraine sufferers, although specific hormonal treatment has been tried.

The Pill with its addition of hormones can also aggravate migraine. This was particularly true in the early days of the pill, when the level of oestrogen and progesterone were greater than they are in present-day preparations. The pill does not cause migraine, it merely lowers the threshold for attacks. Some women experience their first attack soon after starting the pill, but they would probably have developed migraine anyway. It may take several months after starting the pill before a worsening of attacks is seen. Similarly, on discontinuing the pill it may take many months before an improvement occurs. The pill nowadays does not commonly aggravate migraine but when it does it should be discontinued, particularly in classical migraine where it can produce complications, and these questions should be discussed with the doctor or family planning clinic.

Hormone replacement therapy may be necessary for some people, and it could aggravate migraine. There is no way of predicting whose symptoms will be worsened by hormonal treatment, but when this occurs a decision has to be made as to which is the more troublesome condition, hot flushes or migraine. The general practitioner will again advise in such cases.

Pregnancy can improve migraine and has been known to ease it completely, particularly during the third to ninth months. Rarely, migraine may start during pregnancy, and there is sometimes a relapse soon after delivery.

Sleep can trigger migraine. Many sufferers find that they are unwell or have a headache if they lie-in and the symptoms may progress into a migraine. Others may find that too little sleep, particularly if spanning a few nights, may result in an increased frequency of migraine, while many people find that their migraine invariably starts on wakening.

The relationship with the sleep/wakening cycle is not well understood, but the type of sleep that occurs when dreaming (rapid eye movement or REM sleep) seems particularly likely to trigger an attack. There may be a relationship with the pineal gland — a small gland in the brain — which is influenced by the day/night cycle.

In contrast, sleep may often be the most effective treatment for some attacks.

External environment

Stress is the most common precipitant of migraine, even though migraine does not usually occur at the time of the stress but after it. The word stress here covers all recognised varieties of mental stress, such as anxiety, overwork, worry and excitement. It is particularly important as a trigger factor in those people who also experience tension headache, while it is comparatively less important in classical migraine. Perhaps two-thirds of sufferers say that stress is an important factor in triggering their migraine. Stress occurs in everyone's life and it is a normal feature which keeps us awake, but in some people's lives it is excessive or else they respond excessively, both these situations being produced or aggravated by the personality make-up of the sufferer.

A common time for migraine to occur is when winding down, whether it be towards the end of the week, the weekend, or the beginning of a holiday. Other people find that if their stress continues for months they may be migraine free but, as easier times return, so does their migraine.

Particularly in children, it is excitement that is the precipitant. Many look forward to an exciting event but on the big day itself they find they have a migraine.

Occasionally it is physical stress that sets off the attack, e.g. after a game of squash or rugby, or following jogging.

Bright light, loud noise or strong smells can all trigger migraine. Sensitivity to glare is common amongst migraine sufferers. Sometimes it is the glare off water or snow, the sun flickering through the trees whilst driving or the lights in the cinema that are responsible.

Light shines directly on to the back of the eye, stimulating the light-sensitive nerves; the stimulus then passes directly into the brain, where images are constructed. It seems probable that such migraine attacks result from nervous-tissue stimulation. Sound and smell likewise feed straight into the brain and both may also trigger migraine, although loud noise is not a common trigger. Strong smells such as perfume or other volatile liquids may occasionally set off an attack.

strong smells such as perfume or other volatile liquids may occasionally set off an attack.

Climate is yet another migraine trigger. Hot humid weather is often said to cause a migraine, while a few people claim stormy weather invariably precipitates their attack. Hot, stuffy, smoky atmospheres may also set off migraine.

Food as a migraine trigger is a controversial area. Books have been written claiming that the right diet can cure

49

migraine, but this is not strictly true — there is *no* cure for migraine, as it is a result of the effect of environmental factors upon predisposed individuals. Some attacks can be *avoided* but there is no guaranteed cure. Of course everyone wants to find a tangible cause for attacks, with the hope that by avoiding the cause they will no longer get migraine, and there is no more tangible substance than food. Furthermore, food allergy is fashionable and more respectable than admitting to symptoms of anxiety, depression or of excessive stress.

A wide variety of foods may set off migraine — food probably accounts for about 10 per cent of migraine attacks. The trouble is, we have little scientific proof and it is only by the use of scientific verification that we can be sure of something.

The most commonly implicated food factors are alcohol, chocolate, cheese and citrus fruits, and the quantity of each required to precipitate an attack appears to vary considerably from person to person.

Experiments have shown that red wine triggers migraine in some people, usually within 12 hours of consumption. Port and fortified wines may act similarly.

Experiments have shown that red wine triggers migraine in some people.

Alcohol in general may also set off an attack — often quite small amounts are sufficient to trigger it.

Chocolate is perhaps the next most commonly-proclaimed provoking factor and is currently under investigation in scientific trials. Whilst it is unlikely that so many people can be wrong, there is, at present, little evidence that chocolate does cause migraine.

Cheese, particularly strong cheese, appears to be a trigger, while in some people dairy products in general seem to set off attacks.

Fruits like oranges, lemons and grapefruit may trigger attacks. Not only are the fresh fruits important but also soft drinks and flavourings based on them.

Other foods mentioned as trigger factors, include nuts, pork, tomatoes, fried foods and wheat. Missing meals can also be a trigger factor for migraine attacks.

The terms menstrual migraine, weekend migraine and dietary-precipitated migraine have arisen. They are not different conditions but simply migraine triggered by different factors.

HOW DOES MIGRAINE OCCUR?

Just as people vary, so too do migraine sufferers. Some have very frequent attacks (two per week), others only maybe once in their lifetime. Trigger factors have to reach a certain threshold stimulus before they can set off an attack. Some trigger factors may in their own right be powerful enough to set off an attack at any time, e.g. red wine, but most people find that their attacks are as a result of the summation of various trigger factors, e.g. some women can drink red wine provided it is not at the time of their periods. This concept of summation of trigger factors is based purely on clinical experience. With such a diversity in the trigger factors which provoke migraine, is there anything in common between them? All these stimuli might be enough to cause a headache in people not susceptible to migraine; that is, they are generally unpleasant, noxious stimuli which may interfere with our routine daily activity. But why can they cause a migraine attack in susceptible individuals?

Much research has gone into the study of the changes that occur in a migraine attack, and the two main current theories explaining migraine are the vascular theory and the neural theory.

The vascular theory

The pulsatile throbbing nature of the headache in migraine would appear to fit in with a vascular cause for the pain, i.e. a cause originating in the blood circulatory system. Sometimes compression of the neck arteries may relieve the pain felt in the head, again fitting in with this concept. Furthermore, drugs, like ergot, which act on blood vessels can abort a migraine attack, suggesting that vascular changes play an important role in the pathogenesis of migraine, whilst drugs that relax blood vessels, e.g. alcohol, make the pain worse.

It has been proposed that the events occurring before the headache (the aura) were due to constriction of the arteries supplying blood to the brain and the subsequent headache resulted from distension or dilatation of the arteries in the scalp. There is evidence to support both these phenomena, but whether these vascular changes are the cause or the result of the events that occur in migraine remains uncertain. Furthermore, these changes do not explain why the headache is usually one-sided, why some people's attacks are very similar each time, or why the symptoms of migraine are not seen in other conditions where vascular changes occur within the brain, e.g. strokes.

Another hypothesis incorporates the belief that platelets (the clotting particles in blood) are abnormal in people with migraine and are responsible for the attack. Platelets contain a substance called 5-hydroxytryptamine (5-HT) which is capable of constricting blood vessels when released into the circulation upon platelet aggregation. There is evidence that platelets do aggregate during a migraine attack, but this may be a secondary phenomenon.

The neural theory

At the other end of the scale is the neural hypothesis, which proposes that migraine is due to a primary dysfunction of the brain tissue itself and, when a certain threshold is exceeded, an attack follows due to a temporary nervous-tissue abnormality.

This theory fits in well within clinical observations. A disturbance in one cerebral hemisphere could produce one-sided symptoms and a one-sided headache. It explains why light and smells, which feed directly into the brain, can set off an attack within minutes. It also explains why changes in the body's cyclical rhythms can have a direct effect on the frequency of migraine attacks.

Evidence for and against these theories is extensive, but there have been recent studies of blood flow to the brain during a migraine attack, using a radio-isotope tracer method. In common migraine there is no change in blood flow to the brain at any stage of the attack, whilst in classical migraine there is decreased blood flow during the aura phase but no increased blood flow in the headache phase. Furthermore, clinical evidence shows that there is dilatation of blood vessels of the scalp during the headache phase, and they are probably also inflamed.

The brain is able to control the amount of blood it receives, as would be expected in such an important organ. It is therefore likely that migraine will eventually be shown to be primarily a disorder of the nervous system, with secondary vascular changes producing the headache.

Relationship of migraine to other conditions

Migraine is a very common disorder and so will often, just by chance, be associated with other conditions and other causes of headache. There are many ways in which a migraine can be triggered; occasionally, for example, it can be set off by minor head injuries — there is a type of

53

common migraine termed footballer's migraine because it is triggered by heading the ball. However, it is exceedingly rare for migraine to be set off by an underlying brain abnormality; it will only occur in people predisposed to migraine and be associated with other features which make the diagnosis clear.

Links have been noted between epilepsy and migraine. The neurological symptoms of migraine and epilepsy are recurrent and between attacks of each there is complete normality. Whilst migraine is primarily a nervous-tissue disorder, there are far more differences than similarities between these conditions and any link between the two is slight.

Allergic conditions such as asthma, eczema and hay fever have also been linked to migraine, but there is no evidence that this is the case. Nor is there any evidence that migraine is an allergic condition in the accepted medical use of the term.

5.
SELF-HELP

The key word to self-help for any migraine sufferer is 'understanding'. The first stage towards treatment is to understand the condition, which means realising what symptoms can occur as part of the migraine process and understanding how migraine differs from the many other causes of headache. Only after understanding what varieties of factors may precipitate attacks can the search for the causes of migraine begin, whilst an understanding of the different migraine treatments is required before the most suitable one can be chosen. And only when scientists have a better understanding of migraine can more specific treatments be developed.

When a migraine attack occurs, understanding is required by family, friends and employers. Every sufferer has their own way of coping with the problem, and many discover their own self-help ideas, both for migraine attacks as well as for migraine prevention. Certain procedures are almost universally helpful while others may help only a few.

FOR THE MIGRAINE ATTACK

Migraine inevitably interrupts both family and working life. At home it is almost impossible to lie down and rest if there are young children who need constant attention, and repeated attacks strain relationships both at work and at home. An understanding spouse who can look after the family if required is a great comfort; it can be particularly helpful to ask the spouse to attend any medical consultations so that the problem can be shared. It is more difficult to get young children to appreciate a parent's symptoms — a useful trick is to put a band-aid plaster on the forehead during an attack, as children can often identify this with pain and injury and will then become more considerate. In a large company there will inevitably be other sufferers with similar problems; many employers are aware of the problems migraine causes and may have sick bays where people can rest and have treatment.

It is almost impossible to lie down and rest if there are young children who need constant attention.

Treatment for migraine attacks should start as soon as possible and any warning symptoms must be taken as an indication that it is time to start treatment. Many sufferers are compelled to leave work and lie down at home but often, because they cannot think clearly at this time, require someone to help them. It is therefore wise to make precautionary arrangements well in advance, perhaps having a reciprocal understanding with a fellow migraine sufferer. In London, two migraine clinics offer

56

treatment for an attack and usually an intramuscular injection of a painkiller and a drug to control nausea is given and often proves remarkably effective.

At home a dark, quiet place for rest and sleep is required. Thick curtains, eye pads and ear plugs can be helpful and a bowl near the bed for being sick into is often a necessity. Many find a hot water bottle, not too hot, is useful when held to the site of pain, while, in contrast, others prefer to use ice packs; some people even use both. Cold acts like a local anaesthetic and also tends to constrict the large scalp arteries and hence reduce the pain. Heating the small blood vessels of the scalp makes them dilate and this allows blood to flow out of the tender large arteries, while a warm pack behind the neck also helps to relax tense muscles. Always be careful of extremes of temperature which may damage the skin if the sufferer falls asleep.

If an ice pack is used it is best to have two so that one can be left to cool in the refrigerator while the other is being used. Most people prefer not to freeze the packs because they then become stiff and rather uncomfortable.

Sometimes a hot shower or a warm bath will provide comfort by relaxing tense muscles at the beginning of the attack, and some find a warm shower followed by a cold shower is helpful. A V-shaped pillow which fits snugly into the neck can be useful, supporting the head and allowing the neck to relax while lying down.

It is advisable to keep drugs for treatment at home, in the car and at work; it is no good if they are not available when an attack occurs. Only occasionally, for severe attacks, is an injection required from a GP or district nurse.

The physical methods are often a great help in relieving the pain of an attack, but the correct mental approach is vitally important. Many sufferers, when they realise an attack is pending, become depressed, others tend to panic, while some find the symptoms so severe that they are unable to concentrate on anything else. In all situations it is best not to fight migraine but to withdraw completely, relax as much as possible and go to sleep — it must never be forgotten that the disturbance is only temporary.

PREVENTING MIGRAINE

There is no other way of establishing what trigger factors are important in precipitating migraine than by keeping a record and looking for a pattern, it being preferable to make a chart rather than diary notes. For frequent attacks it is worth keeping a daily record, which will probably reveal that a combination of trigger factors sets off an attack rather than a single factor. If there is uncertainty over the nature of the headache, or a possibility of tension headache as well, this chart can be expanded to include the symptoms experienced and then shown to the doctor so that, together, the correct diagnosis will be reached.

There will be many people who still remain uncertain about the cause of their attacks, sometimes because they have concentrated their search in the external environment, perhaps believing that the cause is dietary rather than due to internal triggers such as stress, which are generally not considered quite so acceptable. There is no doubt that many people with frequent migraine (weekly attacks) do have inner anxiety or depression, which themselves may require treatment.

Food

Many migraine sufferers find they are more likely to have an attack when they miss meals. Some find migraine attacks really are closely related to eating, and can prevent attacks by eating smaller but more regular meals. It is best not to go for more than five hours between meals, and a snack last thing at night can be a good idea. Avoiding alcohol, chocolate, cheese and citrus fruits is worth a trial for a few weeks and is not too difficult. For example, carob, available from health food stores, tastes very much like chocolate and can be substituted for it. However, to be sure a particular food is a trigger factor, not only does it have to be omitted from the diet, giving relief from the symptoms; it also has to be reintroduced, with a subsequent worsening of the migraine. Most migraine attacks are in fact due to a combination of trigger factors, and this makes their analysis often difficult.

Medical diets called elimination diets have been evaluated in the prevention of migraine and have received favourable reports, but the trials involved specially selected patients and the diets, apart from being difficult to adhere to, could produce marked weight loss without strict medical supervision. Dramatic changes in eating habits are *not* recommended as a way of looking for a solution to migraine.

Light and eyes

Excessive light is an important trigger factor for migraine and there are several ways of minimising its effects. In the office, try moving the desk to avoid facing a bright light or direct sunlight, change white writing paper to cream or some other softer colour and try to avoid harsh fluorescent lighting. Visual display units (VDUs) are commonly used in offices now and usually have a light intensity control, which can be helpful. At home a soft warm decor is preferable and dimmer switches to control the lighting are a good idea. Colour televisions can be adjusted for contrast and brightness to reduce the intensity of the picture. Light-polarising sunglasses can also be helpful when worn outdoors on sunny days, while the glare from night-driving can be diminished by wearing glasses tinted light yellow or pink.

Most people who develop migraine have their eyes tested, thinking this may reveal the cause of their attacks, but it seldom does. However, those who wear contact lenses may find it more comfortable to remove them during an attack.

Travel

Long journeys can disrupt sleep and meals, as well as

being stressful. Plan ahead and break the journey. Ensure you have an adequate supply of medication. A 'to whom it may concern' letter from your physician is a good idea when going to a foreign country, particularly if you have ever been accused of being drunk or on drugs while having a migraine aura.

Ensure you have an adequate supply of medication.

Atmosphere

Hot, stuffy, smoky atmospheres are to be avoided, as many people find they set off migraine attacks. De-ionisers help remove smoke (but deposit it on the walls and floor) and are said to improve the atmosphere around electrical appliances such as computers and transformers.

Exercise

Regular exercise tones up the cardiovascular (heart and blood supply) system and helps to prevent migraine, but strenuous exercise to which you are unaccustomed should be avoided. Migraine which follows vigorous exercise can sometimes be avoided by drinking a glass or two of water beforehand.

IDENTIFYING A PATTERN

Most people seen in specialist migraine clinics have had many attacks of migraine, and they have identified some sort of pattern to the complaint. Occasionally, however, people have had only one attack, and this first attack usually brings specific problems.

The first attack
This is often an alarming time, people invariably fearing the worst. This is to be expected. One colleague recently had a first attack of classical migraine, which included loss of speech. She was admitted to hospital, had a brain scan and was about to have a lumbar puncture when the consultant arrived and told her she had migraine and could go home. No doubt there are hundreds of similar stories. They all reflect an understandable concern that the symptoms may be due to something serious. However, once it has been termed 'only migraine', medical interest often wanes. The point is that the first line of treatment is to explain and reassure.

Frequent attacks
In this situation we need to look at both predisposing and triggering factors.

PREDISPOSING FACTORS

It is worth enquiring within the family whether anyone else has migraine. While nothing can be done about genetic make-up, it is reassuring to know that there are other family members (and there usually will be one) who have the same problem and with whom the condition can be discussed. Personality should also be considered as it can have an important influence on migraine.

Some people with severe migraine have a lot of anxiety, stress and worry and have difficulty relaxing. Psychologists are experts at this type of problem and are able to advise such patients on ways of relaxing.

TRIGGER FACTORS

People with migraine often ask for tests to see why they get migraine, but there is only one way to look for environmental or trigger factors and that is by keeping a diary, as discussed in the previous chapter.

There is only one way to look for trigger factors and that is by keeping a diary.

When looking for trigger factors there are some important points to remember:

- It is unusual to find a single trigger factor — they are often multiple.
- Most migraine attacks start in the morning and people wake up with them. The reason for this is not known.
- There is often some seasonal variation in migraine.
- Some people find their attacks occur in cycles, with several attacks in succession and none in the following months. Again, the reason for this is not known.

All this makes the search for particular trigger factors more difficult. If attacks are infrequent a diary should be kept of the events at each attack; with frequent attacks it is best to keep a daily diary of events. Not all headaches are due to migraine, and tension headache may be present as well.

Trigger factors can be divided into three groups — avoidable, partly avoidable and unavoidable.

Avoidable trigger factors

The aim of any migraine sufferer is to find the trigger factor for their attacks; by avoiding this trigger, no more attacks should occur. In practice this is not often achieved. Even where a trigger factor is avoidable it is not always humanly possible to omit it completely.

Sleep. Some people are able to avoid their weekend migraine by setting their alarm clocks for the same time as during the week. It is advisable to avoid too many late nights in a row. If you are a very poor sleeper then a short period of night sedation might be advised by the GP, in order to get you into the habit of sleep again.

some people are able to avoid their weekend migraine by setting their alarm clocks for the same time as during the week.

Food. By observing the patterns of migraine, some foods may be discovered to be trigger factors. If no such foods are apparent it is worth omitting alcohol, chocolate, cheese and citrus fruits from the diet for a few months to see if there is any difference. Some brave people even eat amounts of chocolate and cheese or citrus fruits, just to see if these do set off migraine. It is one way — albeit stoical — of really getting at the cause. If there is no relationship to these four major foods then it is unlikely that one will ever be found that makes much difference to your migraine. And remember that eating regular meals is also helpful.

The pill. There is no doubt that the oral contraceptive pill can aggravate migraine. Some people say their attacks started soon after starting the pill, while for others, it may take several months for the pill to worsen migraine attacks. Not only can the attacks be more severe, they can also be more frequent.

Anyone on the pill with frequent migraine should consider coming off it for, say, six months to see if there is any improvement, although this may take up to several months to become apparent. If neurological symptoms start developing while on the pill, your GP will advise on discontinuing the pill.

Hormone replacement therapy may aggravate migraine. In which case it should be discussed with your GP as to whether it ought to be discontinued, especially if frequent migraine occurs.

Partly avoidable trigger factors

Stress. Everyone has experienced stress, but it is difficult to define it. In general terms, stress implies a sense of urgency about actions. In such a situation the mind is alert, the body tensed ready for quick action, and the effect is not necessarily unpleasant. Some people even thrive on stress, which may merely be a result of having a lot to do in a short time. In this familiar situation no single task in itself is stressful — it is just the sheer volume of work that creates the stress. The apparent solution may be to work through lunchtime and to take work home. Many migraine sufferers in fact do not know when to relax, and drive themselves hard.

On the other hand, stress may result from a single specific problem or threatening situation, for example, family problems or shortage of money. Here there is an urgency about resolving the problem; unless a solution is found, the stress remains. Without this sense of urgency there is little stress; being relaxed is having no urgency, with all the time in the world. Excitement is another form of stress, when we look forward with urgency to a pleasant event.

It is in these more specifically stressful situations that anxiety occurs. However anxiety is also as much a reflection of personality as of the stressful situation — what is stressful for one person may not be so for another. Anxiety may be generalised ('upset by everything') or else specific to a particular event. The treatment is to resolve the specific stress factor. If the anxiety is generalised, though, the whole personality needs to be considered in treatment.

Mental and physical relaxation are complementary since the mind and body are in close harmony. A fit body is more able to cope with stress and a fit mind finds solutions to specific problems more easily. The worry of organic illness, of recurring migraine and general physical disability during the migraine attack, erodes the sufferer's mental and physical fitness.

Specific worries need specific treatment, while generalised increased worry needs an overall new approach to stress and its causes, and this is where relaxation programmes in various forms can be very helpful. There are many different approaches to relaxation — in general, both physical and mental ones are used. The close association of mind and body is utilised in this approach and the relaxation programmes aim to decrease the sense of urgency.

A fit body is more able to cope with stress.

Unavoidable trigger factors

Menstruation. Some women have migraine attacks only at the time of menstruation but many more find their migraines are worse around this time. Sometimes an attack also occurs at mid-cycle, the time of ovulation. The pre-menstrual syndrome is poorly understood, and is sometimes difficult to treat effectively. Mental stress is a common feature of this syndrome and of course will aggravate migraine.

Many treatments have been advocated including vitamin B_6 and oil of evening primrose but they are, in general, not very helpful.

6.
NON-DRUG TREATMENT

There is a bewildering array of both drug and non-drug treatments advertised and marketed as being beneficial for the migraine sufferer. Some of these are suggested as treatment for the attack itself, while others are supposed to prevent migraine from starting. Such a mixture of therapies merely reflects the fact that no single treatment is suitable for all sufferers. What works for one person may not work for another. Some treatments are of proven use, while the benefits of others are very dubious.

Just as there are many causes for migraine, so too there are many treatments which are helpful, but finding and treating the cause should be the first aim. Each patient is an individual who requires individual treatment, and while drug treatment of migraine has a great impact, it is not the complete answer.

Any treatment plan for migraine must consider the following:

- There is no cure for migraine, which is the clinical expression, in a predisposed individual, of an abnormal reaction or response to a variety of internal or external stimuli. A predisposed person always remains a predisposed person, but the clinical expression can change and be changed. Migraine is thus not a disease in the usual meaning of the word.
- Migraine is dependent on predisposing factors (inheritance, personality) and trigger factors. Both must be considered in any form of treatment.

67

- There is seldom one single trigger factor responsible for migraine attacks; they are usually produced by a combination of several factors.
- Migraine is a variable condition and improvements for long periods may occur just by chance.
- Whatever form of treatment is taken it is most important that its effects should not be worse than the condition being treated.

Alternative medicine is a widely-used form of therapy for migraine. It is sometimes called complementary medicine to emphasise that it can be used alongside orthodox medicine — it is not necessarily competing with it. The fundamental difference between the two approaches is that orthodox medicine is based on the scientific study of disease, its cause and its treatment. Scientific specialities like pathology, epidemiology, radiology and pharmacology enable us to have a clear understanding of the nature of many diseases, why they occur and how they may be treated. Drugs can be tested in trials — if successful they can be proved to be useful. This approach has enabled us to make enormous strides improving the health of individuals in society. However, orthodox medicine does not have all the answers and while solutions to old problems like migraine continue to be elusive, there will always be alternative therapies.

MEDITATION

There are many types of meditation, but in all of them, the meditator focuses or concentrates his attention or awareness. In visual concentration the focus is on an image, e.g. a flower, while in other forms of meditation, a chant or prayer may be the focus. Whatever the focus, it is said to allow the non-dominant hemisphere of the brain to be at the centre of consciousness, rather than the analytical, ego-centred dominant hemisphere. This decreases heart rate and blood pressure and produces other features seen in the relaxed state.

In visual concentration the focus is an image e.g. a flower, in mental concentration a chant or prayer may be the focus.

RELAXATION PROGRAMMES

Progressive neuromuscular relaxation
This consists of a series of exercises involving contraction and then relaxation of selected muscles in a regulated manner in order to produce a state of deep relaxation. The difference between tension and relaxation can be learnt in this way.

Yoga
This is another way of relaxing the mind and body. It can be easily done at home since there are many easy-to-follow books on this subject.

EXERCISE

Keeping the blood system toned up and developing the ability to relax are both important aspects in the treatment of migraine, and often go hand in hand with pleasurable exercises. Walking is the most popular hobby in Britain today and is a very good form of exercise and relaxation. However, excessive exercise such as squash, jogging and football can occasionally precipitate migraine.

PSYCHOLOGISTS

Many people have an aversion to seeing a psychologist, thinking they have some odd behaviour that needs analysis. But psychologists often offer anxiety-management programmes which may include breathing training, meditation, biofeedback and psychotherapy. Most large hospitals will certainly have such facilities.

ACUPUNCTURE

This is an ancient Chinese art consisting of the insertion of needles at specific points on the body in order to treat disease and to relieve pain. It is an essentially painless procedure and perhaps the most respected of alternative therapies, becoming more and more popular amongst medical practitioners.

Two forms of acupuncture are in current use. One, the traditional method of needle insertion, is based on old traditional Chinese principles of diagnosis and disease classification. The second is a modified method, used usually by doctors in conventional medicine, which places a greater emphasis on painkilling effects. Acupuncturists insert stainless steel needles, perpendicularly or obliquely, to various depths in the skin. The needle point is then stimulated by rotation or by applying an electric current for 10 to 20 minutes.

There are two views on the way acupuncture may work. Traditional Chinese philosophy holds the view that a vital essence, Chi, which is a blend of opposing yin and yang elements, courses through channels under the skin, termed meridians. An imbalance between yin and yang can, it is claimed, be corrected by acupuncture. The acupuncturist examines the patient's tongue, skin, breathing and pulse in order to classify the disease, and

70

then decides on which points on which meridians to stimulate.

Conventional medicine believes acupuncture produces certain painkilling effects mainly by stimulating neurochemical mediators, termed endorphins, found within the body. These are morphine-like compounds which have an effect on pain.

Controlled trials are few in chronic painful conditions, but about 10-15 per cent of patients whose condition does not respond to conventional therapy do claim acupuncture brings relief. However, it is uncertain how effective it is in migraine. Remember, however, acupuncture is not without hazard, since hepatitis has been passed from one person to another through infected needles, and AIDS can theoretically be transmitted in this way.

TRANSCUTANEOUS ELECTRICAL NERVE STIMULATION (TENS)

TENS is a method for relieving pain similar, in principle, to acupuncture, but uses electrodes placed on certain parts of the skin, rather than the insertion of needles, to produce the analgesic effect. An electrical pulse of variable strength and frequency is passed through the electrodes, stimulating nerves in the skin which then alter the pain-controlling mechanism in the spinal cord and also increasing the production of endorphins. TENS has been used to treat many painful conditions but its efficacy in the treatment of migraine is not established.

AROMATHERAPY

This form of alternative therapy involves the inhalation, ingestion or, most commonly, the massaging into the skin of plant-derived oils. This method pays little attention to the diagnosis and is aimed principally at treating symptoms. However, the oils, and hence the treatments, tend to be expensive.

An electrical pulse of variable strength and frequency is passed through the electrodes to stimulate nerves in the skin.

HERBALISM

Practitioners of this form of treatment believe that only plant-derived material should be used in therapy. Herbal medicine is based on the idea of promoting one's own body's healing processes. Medicine is given in small doses (not as small as homeopathic doses) over a short period of time, and there is a wide range of symptom-treating preparations available for self-medication. Lay people often believe that such timed-honoured natural medicines must be safe.

Medical herbalists choose locally grown plants, prepare their own medicines and accept responsibility for their recommendations. Although they can practise without any form of qualification, some are also medically qualified. The National Institute of Medical Herbalists offers a four-year course for lay people and a one-year course for doctors, but relatively few people consult these trained specialists, most going instead to pharmacies, health-food shops and department stores. There are problems over standardisation of the different preparations, and analysis of the various feverfew preparations (see below) have shown marked differences in dosage and quality. This does make assessment of their effectiveness very difficult.

It must be pointed out that many conventional medicines were derived from plant extracts, e.g. codeine and morphine from the poppy, digoxin from the foxglove.

Feverfew (*Tanacetum parthenium*)

This is a weed that has long been held to be useful in the treatment of headache and migraine. Clinical trials have attempted to assess the benefit of feverfew in the prevention of migraine and there is some evidence that it can be useful. Unwanted side effects can include mouth ulceration and a swollen tongue. The leaf itself has a bitter taste but many people grow the plant themselves and take five small leaves a day in a sandwich.

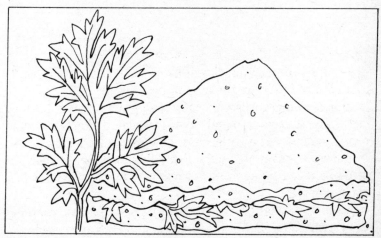

Feverfew – take five small leaves a day in a sandwich.

HOMEOPATHY

This form of therapy has no rational explanation, it being based on what is known as the potency theory. Remedies are made by the process of alternative serial dilution and succussion. Succussion involves partly filling a container with drug, diluent and air and then shaking violently — traditionally by striking the container rhythmically against leather, or the palm of the hand, but nowadays more usually in a mechanical shaker. This is supposed to increase the activity of the drug, a process called potentisation — such products are then called potencies. By this method inactive substances are claimed to become active and active ones more active.

HYPNOTHERAPY

Although everyone has seen or heard of people being hypnotised, little is known about the hypnotic state. Hypnosis should be done only by medical practioners,

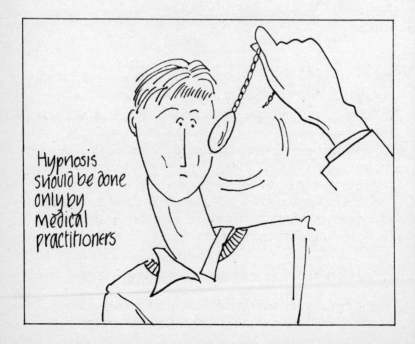

dentists and trained and qualified clinical psychologists. There is some evidence that hypnotheraphy can be useful in the treatment of migraine.

MANIPULATION, OSTEOPATHY AND CHIROPRACTIC

Orthodox medicine regards manipulation as but one of a range of approved treatments that include physiotherapy, anti-inflammatory techniques and surgery, and would restrict manipulation merely to the treatment of pain arising from spinal disorders.

In contrast, a specific concept of disease arising from subluxations or movements of joints is common to both chiropractic and osteopathy, with a distinction that chiropractic defines subluxation as almost the exclusive cause. Though their methods of detection differ, the treatment is essentially the same.

About 2000 lay osteopathic manipulators exist in Britain, but only some hundreds are registered as having had formal instruction. The effectiveness of this form of treatment in migraine is unknown.

REFLEXOLOGY

Practitioners of reflexology use a form of compression massage of the feet of their patients both to diagnose and treat a wide range of conditions. The theories of reflexology therapy were developed by Dr William Fitzgerald in the early 1900s. He described how the body could be divided into ten equal vertical zones, ending in the ten fingers and toes. The zones in the feet are claimed to have direct energy connections with the organs, and treatment involves massage of the relevant zones.

WHY TURN TO ALTERNATIVE MEDICINE?

These forms of alternative medicine all differ in their concepts and theories of disease and its treatment. When doctors cannot see how something can conceivably work on the principles of orthodox medicine, they find it difficult to suggest it as a form of treatment. For example, it is simply not possible for orthodox scientists to accept that a medicine so dilute that it does not even contain so much as one molecule of the remedy in the given dose can have any pharmacological action. Why therefore do so many people turn to alternative medicine in the treatment of migraine?

More than a million people a year seek the help of alternative practitioners, for a variety of conditions. GP consultations, by necessity, are often short, with some limited to five minutes. It is not possible to deal adequately with headache or migraine problems in this short period of time, since migraine is a complicated subject and has many possible causes and many treatments are available. In contrast, alternative medicine therapists in general do spend a comparatively long time with their patients, and quite naturally many people with migraine are attracted to this. There is a large placebo response in any form of migraine treatment. The placebo response (from the Latin, meaning I please) is the finding that if it is really believed that something is going to work, then in some cases it will. For example, if someone is given an inactive drug in the hope that it will improve their migraine, then we know it will do so in 30-40 per cent of cases. This benefit is not permanent, lasting only a matter of weeks or months, depending on the strength of the belief that the treatment is going to be beneficial.

There is a feeling amongst non-migraine-suffering lay people that migraine is not a physical condition. Sufferers therefore, feel guilty that they have migraine and guilty when they have to take time off work or hide themselves away in their bedrooms for one or two days until the attack subsides. Many do not want their family to know that they are suffering, and many do not even bother to consult their general practitioner. Apart from painkillers available from the chemist, there is only alternative medicine left. There is much ignorance amongst sufferers and even amongst some doctors about what treatments are of proven value in migraine.

In conclusion, it is not known how effective alternative medicine is in the treatment of migraine but it may be no greater than that expected of a placebo. Nevertheless, alternative medicine practitioners do take time with their patients and are considerate, and many people gain benefit from this. However, some sufferers try all sorts of alternative treatments, often at great expense, without having tried orthodox medicine. Such an approach is wrong. Only orthodox medicine will give the scientific solution to migraine, and since at present it offers the most effective treatment, it should be tried first.

7.
DRUG
TREATMENT

The first line of treatment for migraine is to define particular trigger factors and avoid them if possible, or modify behaviour if they are stress related. This approach is rational but it is often not an easy form of treatment. Life can be difficult, does have worrying times and many of the pleasurable indulgencies in life encompass migraine triggers. Sometimes migraine occurs for no apparent reason. For all of these reasons, there is an enormous demand for migraine suppression treatment.

There are courses of treatment which can prevent migraine, despite the presence of trigger factors, but any form of treatment must be judged by its effectiveness in the light of safety and lack of side-effects, ease of application and speed of action. The response to treatment should be assessed by a record of attacks, showing their severity and duration.

Some forms of alternative medicine do have a role to play in the treatment of migraine, particularly those concerned with relaxation; on the whole, they are without side-effects. What is unknown in most cases is just how effective they are, and whether orthodox medicine produces a better response. Some forms of alternative medicine cannot be scientifically studied and, in general, we still think that the orthodox approach has the most to offer in the treatment of migraine.

Drugs can have a dramatic impact as a migraine treatment and are used in two ways — in treating the attack once it has started and in the prevention of migraine. Different types of drugs are used in each case.

TREATMENT OF THE ATTACK

No single drug adequately treats each migraine attack, since people vary greatly both in the symptoms requiring treatment and in their response to a given medication. Painkilling and anti-sickness drugs are complementary and usually given together, but finding the most effective combination is sometimes a matter of trial and error. It is unusual not to find significant benefit from these sorts of drugs, but there are certain problems encountered during the drug treatment of the migraine attack:

- Sickness, a very common symptom, prevents the stomach working properly and so tablets are not well absorbed, and can even be vomited up unchanged many hours after they have been swallowed.
- Not all migraine attacks follow the same pattern in each individual. This means that the effect of a treatment cannot be fully assessed after taking it for one attack. It must be taken for several attacks before its effectiveness can be judged.
- As symptoms progress during a migraine attack they may be blamed on the drugs taken earlier.

Medication for the attack is more effective if taken as early as possible — even before the headache if there is a warning signal. Soluble medication acts more quickly than solid because of the greater surface area for absorption and should be used in preference wherever possible, although, when nausea and vomiting are severe, the water needed to dissolve these tablets may itself irritate the stomach and aggravate the situation. Some soluble preparations are available in an efferverscent form and occasionally this gassy fluid may have a similar detrimental effect.

Four main groups of drugs are used for treating the acute attack:

- Painkillers (analgesics)
- Anti-sickness drugs (anti-emetics)
- Combined painkiller and anti-sickness drugs
- Ergot-based drugs

Painkillers

There is a wide variety of different painkillers available for the treatment of migraine. Most over-the-counter painkillers can be helpful, but sometimes drugs on prescription are needed. It is certainly best to try the simpler remedies first, since they are adequate for many sufferers.

Administration by mouth is of course the most common way of taking medication, but some painkillers are formulated for administration under the tongue (sublingually), by rectum (suppository) or else may be given by a nurse or medical practitioner intramuscularly (rarely required). Each method has advantages and disadvantages but the aim in every case is to get the drug to the site of action as quickly as possible.

Five categories of painkiller (analgesic) are used in the treatment of migraine attacks:

- Aspirin
- Paracetamol
- Non-steroidal anti-inflammatory drugs
- Mixed analgesic preparations
- Narcotic analgesics

Aspirin is the most widely used and two tablets (300 mg each) may be taken up to four times a day in adults. Aspirin should not be given as a treatment for headache in children under 12 years old due to the association with a rare liver disease (Reye's syndrome).

Aspirin is generally well tolerated but does occasionally irritate the stomach and should be used with caution in

81

people prone to indigestion. This problem can be minimised by taking the dose after food and in a soluble form (dispersible or effervescent). For attacks with severe vomiting a suppository form can be helpful.

Paracetamol is another widely used painkiller, which can be effective in a dose of two tablets (500 mg each) up to four times a day. Paracetamol has few side effects in this dose and many different preparations are available. It is suitable for children and may be given in a liquid form (paediatric elixir).

Non-steroidal anti-inflammatory drugs are similar in many ways to aspirin. This group of drugs affects the production of pain-provoking substances (prostaglandins) in the body. Ibuprofen (Nurofen) is available without prescription. Mefanamic acid (Ponstan, 500 mg three times a day) and diclofenac (Voltarol, 25 to 50 mg three times a day) are the most commonly prescribed. Some are available in suppository form. Diclofenac (Voltarol, 75 mg by intramuscular injection) is also used for an acute migraine attack.

Mixed analgesic preparations. There are many different types containing, for example, aspirin, paracetamol and codeine, but in general it is best to keep to single-ingredient preparations. Some mixed preparations contain mild muscle relaxants, and many contain caffeine — a weak stimulant that has no painkilling property but which, in excessive dosage or on withdrawal, may itself induce headache.

Perhaps the most commonly prescribed combination tablets are Co-proxamol (previously called Distalgesic and containing the analgesics paracetamol and dextropropoxyphene), Solpadeine (effervescent tablets containing paracetamol, codeine and caffeine) and Syndol (tablets containing paracetamol, codeine, doxylamine for muscle relaxation and caffeine). Midrid is a combination tablet marketed for both tension headache and migraine (containing paracetamol, dichloralphenazone for relaxation and isometheptene).

Narcotic analgesics are strong painkillers and can be

addictive, so should only be used when absolutely necessary and then sparingly at the direction of the general practitioner. Narcotic analgesics share many side-effects, including constipation, nausea, respiratory depression and cough suppression, and some cause drowsiness. Codeine and dihydrocodeine (DF 118) can be effective in migraine and are the most suitable of the narcotic analgesics. Buprenorphine (Temgesic) has become a popular drug for severe pain as it is not supposed to be addictive and is available in a convenient under-the-tongue (sublingual) formulation, but it has little use in the treatment of migraine and should be avoided. Pentazocine (Fortral) is occasionally prescribed for migraine, but may cause hallucinations and is not recommended. Pethidine is a well-known strong painkiller which is occasionally given by intramuscular injection when the headache is very severe.

Anti-sickness drugs

These are very useful drugs in the treatment of migraine since nausea is almost invariable during an attack. In fact, nausea may be the most severe symptom of the attack and can prevent any form of orally administered drug from being absorbed. There are several useful anti-sickness drugs.

Metoclopramide (Maxolon) is the most useful drug in the prevention of migraine sickness and is usually taken with an analgesic. It is available in 10 mg tablets which may be taken up to three times a day. It seldom has any side effects, although occasionally muscle spasms, drowsiness, constipation, breast enlargement and milk production may occur. Metoclopramide speeds up the absorption of painkillers, thereby making them more effective. Metoclopramide is not available in Britain in suppository form but can be given by intramuscular injection.

Prochlorperazine (Stemetil) is another widely-used anti-emetic but is probably not quite as good as metoclopramide when given orally. It is marketed in oral,

83

rectal and intramuscular preparations; the suppository form is particularly helpful for marked vomiting, and is available in two strengths, 5 mg for children and 25 mg for adults.

Domperidone is an effective anti-sickness drug, also available in suppository form, which, if taken early enough, can prevent the attack from becoming more severe.

Combined painkiller and anti-emetic drugs
Combination tablets containing painkillers and anti-sickness drugs are available, the most popular being Migraleve, Migravess and Paramax.

Ergot-based drugs
The fungus *Claviceps purpurea*, more commonly known as hornseed or mother of rye, grows on the rye plant and produces ergot. Ergot contains a mixture of substances, one of which is called ergotamine and it is this that is used in the treatment of migraine. In Europe during the fourteenth century there were outbreaks of a condition known as St Anthony's Fire, which was due to eating rye bread which had been kept for too long and was contaminated with the *Claviceps purpurea* fungus. Victims would develop an extensive rash, discolouration of their fingers and toes and, in extreme cases, gangrene and putrefaction of their limbs, which would then drop off — 'severed as if by some sudden fire'. We now know that these symptoms were due to the constricting action of ergot on blood vessels but at that time the only known cure was a pilgrimage to the shrine of St Anthony in Italy, a journey which took several months for those from northern parts. Since the journey took the victims out of the endemic area, they no longer ate bread contaminated with ergot and, by the time they reached the shrine, were often cured.

Ergotamine, developed from ergot, became the first drug specifically designed to treat migraine and is still in widespread use. The pain of migraine is associated with distended blood vessels and ergotamine, by constricting them, reduces the headache, although to do so it must be taken early. However, while there is no doubt that ergotamine can be very effective, it should only be used when other, safer, treatments have not worked. Ergotamine-containing preparations can be administered orally, sublingually, rectally, and by inhalation.

There are three main points to bear in mind with drugs containing ergotamine:

- Because they constrict arteries they should never be used if there is arterial disease, e.g. pain in the legs on walking (intermittent claudication), heart disease (coronary artery disease), strokes (cerebrovascular disease).
- There is a strict limit to the number of tablets that can be taken each day and each week. Higher doses can damage normal arteries.
- They are addictive and have to be taken early in the attack to be effective. Many people with a combination of migraine and tension headache find it impossible to distinguish between these two headaches at their onset and so, because tension headache is a frequent type of headache, they should avoid ergotamine-based drugs. Similarly, people with frequent migraine (one attack or more a month) should not rely on ergotamine to treat their attacks, otherwise what may start as frequent migraine which is well treated with ergotamine can turn into ergotamine dependency. In this situation withdrawal symptoms similar to those of migraine occur and, of course, will respond very well to taking more ergotamine.
- Once habituated, it is not easy to get off ergotamine.

Of the various preparations available, the most popular are Cafergot, Migril and Lingraine. They should never be taken on a regular basis for migraine but can be taken prior to any symptoms where migraine attacks occur with a high degree of predictability, e.g. menstrual migraine, migraine triggered by strenuous exercise or intercourse. The correct dosage is the minimum which is found to be effective, and this can be found only by trial and error.

PREVENTATIVE TREATMENT

For people with frequent migraine, preventative treatment is the most logical type of drug therapy and can be effective in a high percentage of people. A number of questions need consideration, however.

There are no hard and fast rules as to those who should try preventative therapy, but anyone with two or more attacks a month should be considered. Two important factors, besides attack frequency, are attack duration and severity (both reflect effectiveness of acute treatment) and the effect that frequent attacks have on daily life. A single severe attack each month which threatens career or work can justify daily treatment, while three brief mild attacks might not. Before embarking on a treatment course which may last several months it is wise to see if the attacks have an established pattern.

The following drugs are all used in the preventative treatment of migraine:

- Betablockers
- Pizotifen
- Methysergide
- Calcium-channel blockers
- Clonidine

While there is extensive information on the actions of all these migraine-preventative drugs, so far no known single property can account for the benefits they produce.

Betablockers
Betablockers (or beta-receptor blockers) are a family of related drugs which have similar actions on blood vessels and the nerves that control them. They slow the heart rate

and lower blood pressure and so are used to treat high blood pressure and some forms of heart disease. In 1966 a patient with heart disease and migraine found that when he was treated with a betablocker called propranolol (Inderal) his migraine attacks were greatly improved, and since then it has been established that propranolol, and certain other betablockers, are very effective in preventing migraine.

The most widely used drug in this group for migraine prevention is still propranolol, and it is now marketed specially for this condition. Its use in such medical conditions as high blood pressure may worry some migraine patients when it is suggested as a migraine treatment, but it is quite common for one drug to be used in two or more different situations, for example aspirin is used primarily as a painkiller but it is also used to prevent strokes, codeine is a useful painkiller but is often used to control diarrhoea.

Betablockers in general (and propranolol in particular), cannot be given to asthmatics, people with heart failure and to some diabetics because they will worsen these conditions, but otherwise they are very safe drugs and thousands of people have been on them for many years continuously without problems (e.g. those with high blood pressure). While all drugs have side-effects, most people taking propranolol each day do not notice any, although occasionally mild transient lethargy can occur, and people prone to cold hands and feet may find that this is worsened.

Equally as important as the appropriate choice of drug is the correct dosage — often too small a dose is given. At the Princess Margaret Migraine Clinic in London the usual starting dose of propranolol is 80 mg each day, although it may occasionally work at lower doses. The 80 mg dose may be taken as 40 mg twice a day, or as a special 80 mg formulation taken once a day, which releases propranolol slowly so that one tablet lasts all day. This slow-release or long-acting (LA) formulation is named Inderal LA, and is taken each morning.

If treatment for high blood pressure is needed as well as for migraine, it is sensible to choose a betablocker that is effective in both conditions.

Pizotifen (Sanomigran)

Pizotifen, developed specifically as a migraine preventative, is technically termed a 5-HT blocker although it also has antihistamine properties. It has an excellent safety record and has been in widespread use for many years, initially at a dose of 0.5 mg three times a day but now more commonly given as 1.5 mg at night. The two side effects that occasionally occur are:

- Drowsiness, which may prevent the continued use of pizotifen, although it is usually mild and wears off in a few days
- Appetite stimulation, which makes people feel hungry, eat more and so put on weight.

appetite stimulation which makes people feel hungry, eat more and so put on weight.

Both side-effects are rapidly reversed by stopping the drug, while its mild sedative effect can be beneficial.

Pizotifen is also available in a liquid preparation for children.

Methysergide (Deseril)

Methysergide is probably the most effective migraine preventative drug and is, like pizotifen, a 5-HT blocker. It is not widely used because it is generally regarded as being less safe than the betablockers or pizotifen. When methysergide was used in long-term treatment there were suggestions that it caused scarring in various organs in the body, so its current use is restricted to a period of three to six months, after which time it should be tailed off and discontinued for one month before re-starting it. A dose of 1 mg two or three times a day is used in migraine but this treatment should be periodically reviewed by the doctor.

Calcium-channel blockers

This family of drugs has a similar mode of action to the betablockers; they all dilate blood vessels by relaxing the muscles in the vessel wall. They are becoming increasingly popular in the prevention of migraine, particularly in America. Like the betablockers they are currently used in Britain for the treatment of high blood pressure and some forms of heart disease but, unlike betablockers, they can be used safely in asthmatics.

Clonidine (Dixarit)

Clonidine was first used in the treatment of high blood pressure and it acts both on blood vessels and within the brain. In smaller doses it is used in the prevention of migraine and is currently the most widely prescribed of the migraine-preventative drugs.

As already emphasised, to prove that a treatment is more useful than a placebo, a double-blind trial must be carried out comparing that treatment with a placebo. These trials are not easy to perform in a condition like migraine and so doctors like to see evidence from several trials before deciding whether the treatment will be useful or not. However, it is now clear that Dixarit is of little use as a migraine preventative.

Migraine-preventative drugs do not work immediately. It usually takes several weeks before their effects become apparent, and it may be two months before an adequate time has passed for proper assessment. Once preventative treatment is started it should be continued for at least two months before any changes are made. The drug must be taken every day.

Preventative drugs usually affect both the frequency and the severity of the attacks, although sometimes only one of these factors is affected, for example attacks are unchanged in severity but are much less frequent while others find the opposite. It is not uncommon to find that attacks stop completely for several months at a time, and in this situation the impact on a person's life can be dramatic. If a drug has been given a fair trial both in terms of duration and dosage with little or no improvement, another type of preventative drug should be tried — there is invariably one that will be found helpful.

All currently-available migraine-preventative drugs, apart from methysergide, may, in theory, be continued indefinitely, although this is neither necessary nor desirable. In general, apparently effective treatment should be discontinued after a few months to see if the drug is still needed (i.e. whether the migraine returns or not), although some people are so pleased to find some effective treatment that they prefer to stay on regular medication for a year or more.

When preventative therapy is stopped there is often an appreciable period during which migraine does not reappear. It has been suggested that effective preventative therapy not only trains the blood vessels to respond normally again, thereby lessening the chances of migraine, but, if started early on, also prevents migraine progressing into a more frequent form.

Having found an effective preventative drug the next question is 'Will the benefit continue?' Some people taking daily pizotifen find it loses its beneficial effect after about six months. Similarly, with propranolol migraine can break through after several months of daily medication, although it is more common to find a steady improvement in the longer term. In cases where a fall-off in drug effectiveness with time is seen, adjusting the dosage or changing to another type of migraine-preventative drug will usually restore migraine control.

SPECIAL CONSIDERATIONS

Children
Some children are greatly affected by migraine and this can produce immense stress on the parents and family as a whole. There is a greater reluctance to prescribe preventative drugs for children than for adults, but nevertheless both pizotifen and propranolol can be used with good results, with pizotifen the drug of choice and given in a smaller dose.

Pregnancy
Fortunately it is rare to be troubled by migraine during pregnancy, particularly after the third month, and daily migraine-preventative treatment can be avoided. Although there are unlikely to be any problems if a woman does become pregnant while taking either pizotifen or propranolol, common sense suggests that all drugs should be avoided if pregancy is desired. Paracetamol is perhaps the safest analgesic if one is necessary.

Menstrual migraine
Women who have a migraine attack at a similar or exact time each month can plan their treatment in advance. Initially, particularly when there are warning symptoms before the attack proper, it is best to try treatments usually reserved for the attack itself. Ergotamine-containing preparations are often effective in these situations but the problems inherent with these drugs have to be considered. Propranolol or pizotifen, taken one or two weeks beforehand, can be effective in preventing the attack and are often the most suitable form of therapy.

Ergotamine dependency

People who take ergotamine very frequently may be dependent on it without realising it, since ergotamine is both addictive and has withdrawal symptoms which may mimic a migraine attack. In cases of ergotamine addiction there is no alternative but to stop the ergotamine completely and change to a safer treatment, although it is not always easy to do this immediately. The introduction of a migraine-preventative drug together with increasingly smaller and less frequent doses of ergotamine usually solves this problem.

OTHER USEFUL DRUGS

Amitriptyline

Besides being a useful drug in the treatment of depression, amitriptyline can be taken in addition to propranolol for increased effect in preventing migraine. It often helps the tension headache which is so often seen in association with migraine.

Non-steroidal anti-inflammatory drugs

Although these drugs are usually used to treat a migraine attack (see page 82), some have been shown to prevent migraine when taken daily.

Tranquillisers

The long-term use of tranquillisers must be avoided, but the occasional use of diazepam (Valium) in a highly anxious situation can be beneficial and is quite safe. Its relaxing effect on muscles is an added benefit in those migraine attacks where muscle spasm produces tension headache.

Miscellaneous drugs

People have tried diuretics for menstrual migraine, vitamins, particularly vitamin B_6, oil of evening primrose and hormone treatments with, overall, little benefit.

8.
QUESTIONS AND ANSWERS

What is migraine?

There are many types of headaches but only one occurs in combination with several other symptoms to form a pattern recognised as migraine. It is more than a headache alone, although this is usually the worst symptom, and always occurs in distinct attacks, with complete recovery in between. The symptoms are diverse both in their nature and in their severity, but they are very real and unpleasant — those who do not suffer from the complaint cannot fully appreciate how unpleasant it is.

In a typical attack the patient prefers to lie still in bed, undisturbed, in a quiet darkened room. The patient looks pale and ill, has a severe throbbing headache, feels sick and at times may well be sick, which might relieve the headache. The attacks last from a few hours to several days but are always temporary, often relieved by sleep and followed by complete recovery.

What types of migraine are there?

Several varieties of migraine are recognised, classified on whether or not neurological symptoms occur during the attack. Three broad categories are seen:

- Common migraine — no overt neurological symptoms.
- Classical migraine — neurological symptoms present.
- Migraine equivalent — neurological symptoms but no headache.

Within each category there are several sub-types.

Common migraine — an episodic headache, most commonly unilateral (one-sided), associated with nausea, vomiting, photophobia, phonophobia, osmophobia but not with focal neurological symptoms is termed common migraine. As the name implies, this is by far the most frequent variety of migraine. There is no entirely satisfactory definition and so set criteria are often used in diagnosis; this is particularly important when research studies are undertaken.

The terms menstrual migraine, dietary-precipitated migraine and footballer's migraine are types of common migraine which all have particular triggers. If the pain of a common migraine attack is experienced below the level of the eyes it is called facial migraine (sufferers may erroneously think the pain results from disease of the teeth).

Footballer's Migraine.

Classical migraine — there is great variety within the focal neurological symptoms that can be seen in classical migraine. Attacks in which visual and other focal neurological symptoms precede the headache by some 20-60 minutes and disappear as the headache develops are the most frequent type of classical migraine but other varieties include the following:

- *Vertebrobasilar migraine* — Symptoms referable to the basilar artery territory (see page 19) start before the headache but persist into the headache phase. This variety is seen particularly in adolescent girls.
- *Hemiplegic migraine* — Weakness or paralysis of a limb is uncommon in migraine attacks but occurs in hemiplegic migraine. It may run in families and is then termed familial hemiplegic migraine.
- *Ophthalmoplegic migraine* — Visual symptoms start after the headache phase, continue after the headache has resolved and result from disturbances in the nerves controlling eye movements. It occurs in young children.
- *Retinal migraine* — This very rare variety is thought to be due to constriction of arteries supplying the eye. It produces visual symptoms, but in one eye only.

What are migraine equivalents?

When focal neurological symptoms start, and subside, as expected in a typical classical migraine attack, but no headache follows, the term migraine equivalent is used (see page 96).

Who gets migraine?

There are about 10 million migraine sufferers in Britain, three-quarters are female and a family history is seen in about 70 per cent. Migraine can start at almost any age, but 90 per cent of sufferers have had their first attack before the age of 40. There is no association between migraine and intelligence or social class, but many migraine sufferers are ambitious meticulous people who have difficulty relaxing and are prone to feelings of anxiety.

What triggers migraine attacks?

In predisposed people many different factors can set off an attack, in a way comparable to pulling the trigger of a gun. The major trigger factors are stress (particularly relaxation after stress), hormonal changes (puberty, menstruation and the oral contraceptive pill), interruption of normal sleep patterns, dietary (alcohol, chocolate, cheese and citrus fruits) and physical stimuli like light (particularly glare), noise and smells (e.g. perfume).

How are trigger factors recognised?

The only way to discover what sets off migraine is to look for associations by keeping a record of events (social, work and family), food and drink consumed, sleep, stage of the menstrual cycle, as well as environmental factors (light, glare, noise, weather, atmosphere) surrounding the attack. Most attacks result from a combination of more than one of these trigger factors.

A diary of attacks is worth keeping, including the response to different treatments, since it is difficult to remember the details of each attack if they are frequent.

Is migraine always associated with headache?

The hallmark of a migraine attack is the brain disturbance that occurs, producing warning (prodromal) symptoms within an hour before the headache (disturbances of vision or speech, or pins and needles), premonitory symptoms up to 24 hours before the attack (hunger, lethargy, depression or exhilaration), or the apparent irritability of the brain to stimuli like light, noise or smells. The more focal prodromal symptoms usually occur before the headache and last 20 to 30 minutes, but in some there may be no subsequent headache (these attacks are then called migraine equivalents).

The most common type of migraine equivalent is a visual disturbance which can include flashing lights, zig-zag lines or loss of vision, and it occurs more frequently in older age groups. Abdominal migraine is another type of migraine equivalent, but is seen only in children, who experience recurrent attacks of abdominal pain, nausea and look unwell.

Migraine equivalents usually occur in people who also suffer more typical migraine; in those cases where there is no such history the diagnosis can be difficult.

Are any conditions associated with migraine?

There are several episodic or periodic conditions which may be allied to migraine. These include:

- Vomiting ('bilious') attacks of childhood
- Episodic chest pain ('cardiac migraine')
- Episodic vertigo (benign recurrent vertigo)
- Alternating hemiplegia of childhood

How long can migraine attacks last?

The vast majority last between 2 and 72 hours but some patients say they can feel 'migrainous' for a week at a time, with an almost continuous migraine-like headache and nausea. This situation — status migrainosus — is uncommon and may be related to strong emotional factors and to excessive use of ergotamine and painkilling drugs. It is quite unlike cyclical migraine, where a group of attacks occur close together before going away for long periods of time. It is not uncommon for muscle contraction or tension headache to occur during, or even outlast, a migraine attack.

When should I see a doctor?

Many patients diagnose and treat their own headaches since, in most cases, this is quite straightforward. However if there is doubt about the diagnosis, or treatment is not deemed to be adequate, then advice from a doctor may be required. A survey in the Rhondda Valley in South Wales showed that about 50 per cent of female migraine sufferers had never consulted a doctor for this condition, and it was those from higher social groups that were more likely to seek medical advice.

Are there any tests for migraine?

There are no reliable tests for migraine; the diagnosis depends purely on the pattern of the symptoms, for there will be no abnormality to find on examination. Any tests that a doctor might do are to rule out organic disease in difficult or rare cases (and this is infrequent). Skin tests and the cytotoxic test are of little use in predicting the cause of migraine.

What is migraine due to?

Migraine usually runs in the family and sufferers inherit a predisposition towards it, although quite what these inherited genes are is unknown. Various trigger factors may set off attacks from time to time in those who are predisposed, and it is the body's response that produces the collection of symptoms known as migraine. It is not known what tissue in the body sets off the migraine pathways, but at present the neural theory — that it starts within the brain — is generally favoured.

What changes occur in the body during a migraine attack?

The chemical study of migraine has concentrated on those substances thought to be involved in pain production and regulation, as well as those concerned with the control of blood flow in the brain, e.g. prostaglandins, kinins, endorphins and vasoactive amines which are produced in cells and tissues including the walls of blood vessels, the platelets and in the blood and other blood and nerve cells. During a migraine attack many biochemical changes occur in the body, and blood vessels supplying blood to the brain and scalp may constrict and then dilate. However the precise detail of these changes is unknown.

A primary change in the blood system, causing decreased blood flow to the brain and hence neurological symptoms, seems less likely than a trigger in the nervous system, with secondary vascular changes.

What foods cause migraine?

Of the many foods and drinks implicated in precipitating migraine, only red wine has been proven unequivocally to do so. Alcoholic drinks of any sort are commonly said by sufferers to be migraine triggers, while the commoner foods that are triggers are chocolate, cheese and citrus fruits. Dietary-precipitated migraine accounts for over 10 per cent of all migraine attacks, and although other foods like eggs, wheat, peanuts, pork, tomatoes and yeasts are thought by some sufferers to be triggers, these are not common.

Food and alcohol will precipitate an attack within 12 to 24 hours of consumption but the quantity needed is very variable and usually there is another factor involved.

How do some foods precipitate migraine?

There has been a good deal of interest in a chemical called tyramine (a natural substance found in a range of foods thought to precipitate migraine) and in flavinoids (found in red wine), but there is still no clear answer as to what it is in these foods that is responsible for precipitating a migraine attack.

Is migraine due to food allergy?

Allergy is a medical term that implies the involvement of the immune system (antibodies), but there is no evidence that this system takes any part in precipitating migraine, unlike asthma or hay fever.

Why are women more commonly affected?

It is not known why there are three times as many women sufferers as men. However, since migraine in children is more common in boys, it is likely to be related to the female sex hormones (these hormones being absent in girls until puberty), which might make the blood vessels in the head more sensitive to migraine triggers.

Should the contraceptive pill be taken by those with migraine?

The pill is a migraine trigger which, like chocolate, may be important in some individual cases, but there is no way of predicting, with certainty, whom. Some patients with no history of migraine find that migraine starts soon after going on the pill. However, the pill does not cause migraine, it merely makes it more likely to occur. It is the *falling* level of the sex hormone, oestrogen, in the bloodstream that is important in triggering an attack of migraine rather than the actual level of the hormone. When the pill contained comparatively high doses of oestrogen it commonly worsened migraine, but the combined low-dose oestrogen and progesterone pills used today do so less often. With the current oral contraceptive pills there is little to be gained from changing from one type to another in the hope of finding one that is less likely to aggravate migraine.

A deterioration of migraine in women on the oral contraceptive pill is more likely to occur in older women (particularly those over 30 years), in those with a menstrual cycle length outside 27 to 30 days, where there is a menstrual pattern of migraine and where there is onset of migraine after a pregnancy. It may take several months for the pill to worsen migraine and, similarly, improvement on stopping the pill may not be seen for several weeks.

If there is a worsening of migraine on starting the pill, the pill should be discontinued; if there is a sudden deterioration, with the appearance for the first time of neurological symptoms, it must be stopped immediately and medical advice sought. Some doctors do not prescribe oral contraceptives for sufferers with classical migraine because of the very slight increased risk of complications.

What happens to migraine during pregnancy?

Neary 80 per cent of migraine sufferers find that their migraine attacks improve during pregnancy, with nearly 60 per cent having complete relief, although about 20 per cent find little change and, rarely, attacks can be made worse. The sex of the baby has no influence on the course of migraine during pregnancy.

Is there a safe treatment for migraine during pregnancy?

All drugs are best avoided during pregnancy, but paracetamol is regarded as a safe painkiller that can be used. Migraine has no detrimental effect on pregnancy, despite the severe symptoms that may occur. Some sufferers claim acupuncture can help and it is certainly a safe treatment at this time.

Will migraine be passed on to the children?

Migraine is often a strongly-inherited condition, but there is no simple pattern of inheritance. A positive family history is seen in about 70 per cent of sufferers and is usually on the mother's side. If the father has migraine, there tends to be an earlier age of onset of migraine in his children. There is little tendency for the same type of migraine to run in the family and the trigger factors will also vary in importance between different family members.

One rare type of migraine which causes weakness of one side of the body (hemiplegia), and called familial hemiplegic migraine, affects most family members, has a similar age of onset in each of them and is precipitated by very similar trigger factors.

What is the treatment for migraine in children?

Migraine commonly occurs in children, boys slightly more than girls, common migraine being the most frequently occurring variety. Classical migraine occurs, but less frequently than in adults. Abdominal migraine is a migraine equivalent which occurs only in children. Treatment of these conditions follows the same lines as in adults, and often the preventative drugs propranolol (Inderal) and pizotifen (Sanomigran) are helpful.

Can severe frequent migraine cause lasting damage?

Although the pain of migraine can be very severe, and suggests, at times, that the head is about to 'explode', it causes no permanent damage. Similarly, the neurological symptoms can be pronounced but are transient.

Doctors and psychologists have studied the effects of frequent migraine on both brain structure (using CT scanning, see page 39) and brain function (e.g. testing memory), and there is little difference when compared to a control group.

Very occasionally one hears of someone having a stroke during a migraine attack (i.e. having a permanent neurological symptom, such as limb paralysis) but this is extremely rare and is usually associated with other risk factors for stroke, such as smoking or the oral contraceptive pill.

Are alternative medicines useful in treating migraine?

There has been little scientific study of the benefit of alternative medicine in the treatment of migraine, and in some types of treatment such a study is impossible. It is often difficult, on theoretical grounds, to see how some treatments could work, while those which are aimed particularly at relaxation would be expected to help some people. Orthodox medicine still offers the most effective treatment and should therefore be tried first.

Is feverfew helpful?

Feverfew is a plant which has long been claimed to be helpful in the treatment and prevention of migraine and headache, and there is some evidence to support this view. It may be bought from health shops in commercial preparations, although these may vary in their dosage of active ingredient. Many people grow the plant in their garden or in a flower pot on the window sill and take five small leaves a day, often in a sandwich, since the leaves have a bitter taste. Feverfew appears to be safe when taken in this way but occasionally produces a sore mouth. The substances thought to be active have been analysed and have a chemical structure similar to ergotamine (itself produced by a fungus which affects rye).

What drugs are used to treat migraine?

There are two different ways of using drugs to treat migraine — treating the attack once it has started, and preventing the attack. The types of drug used in each case are different.

Painkillers, often with a drug to treat sickness, are tried first, and only if they are ineffective is ergotamine considered. Soluble preparations work quicker and should be taken early in the attack, before the headache if there is a warning.

For frequent attacks (two or more a month) it is worth considering daily treatment with preventative drugs. These are not painkillers; they block the effect of various substances on blood vessels or have a direct effect on the vessel themselves. They do not work immediately and so should be tried for several weeks before deciding whether or not they are effective. The most widely used are propanolol (Inderal), pizotifen (Sanomigran), clonidine (Dixarit) and methysergide (Deseril). They are usually taken for a few months at a time and then discontinued.

What painkillers are best for migraine?

There is a lot of individual variation, and different painkillers may have to be tried until a suitable one is found. Aspirin or paracetamol are often sufficient, particularly when combined with a drug to combat sickness, and the strong narcotic painkillers are rarely necessary.

Is migraine a true disease?

Migraine is not a disease in the usual meaning of the word; it is a reaction which occurs in predisposed people under certain circumstances. It may be a defence reaction and some believe it is a way of getting rid of inner tensions, although in many its function, if any, is dubious.

What is the natural history of migraine?

There is little information available on the long-term outlook for migraine sufferers. One study followed nearly 100 patients for at least 14 years, and just over 60 per cent were still experiencing attacks at the end of the study, although most had found the attacks had become less frequent or less severe. Of the females in the study who had gone through the menopause, about 60 per cent found their migraines were unchanged, 7 per cent were improved, in 7 per cent attacks had ceased, while 20 per cent were worse.

In general migraine and headache become less troublesome with advancing years.

Is any progress being made in migraine research and treatment?

Research can be compared to the building of a brick wall, where the end result depends on the correct placement of hundreds of individual bricks. A great deal of work, throughout the world, is being done to advance our understanding of migraine, but there are still difficulties which hinder progress, particularly the lack of a widely-accepted definition of migraine, a reliable test and an experimental model.

Research depends on the close cooperation of patient, doctor and scientist and is facilitated by the specialised migraine clinics, which not only give advice but also assess new treatments and are often integrated into research laboratories with high-technology equipment. Those areas of the brain thought to be important in triggering migraine have, until now, been largely inaccessible to study but recent advances in scanning techniques make one optimistic for the future.

USEFUL ADDRESSES

INFORMATION AND ADVICE

United Kingdom
The Migraine Trust
45 Great Ormond Street
London WC1N 3HD
Tel: 01-278 2676

The British Migraine Association
178A High Road
Byfleet
Surrey KT14 7ED
Tel: 09323 52468

Canada
The Migraine Foundation
390 Brunswick
Toronto
Ontario

CLINICS

United Kingdom
Princess Margaret Migraine Clinic
Charing Cross Hospital
Fulham Palace Road
London W6 8RF
Tel: 01-741 7833

City of London Migraine Clinic
22 Charterhouse Square
London EC1M 6DX
Tel: 01-251 3322

National Hospital for Nervous Diseases
Queen Square
London WC1
Tel: 01-837 3611

Birmingham and Midland Eye Hospital
Church Street
Birmingham
Tel: 021-236 4911

Radcliffe Infirmary
Woodstock Road
Oxford OX2 6HE
Tel: 0865 249891

Hull Royal Infirmary
Anlaby Road
Hull
Tel: 0482 28541

Newcastle General Hospital
Westgate Road
Newcastle-upon-Tyne NE4 6BE
Tel: 091 2738811

Adenbrooke's Hospital
Hill's Road
Cambridge CB2 2QQ
Tel: 0223 245151

Royal Devon and Exeter Hospital
Barrack Road
Exeter EX2 5DW
Tel: 0392 77833

Southern General Hospital
Govan Road
Glasgow G51 4TF
Tel: 041-445 2466

Western General Hospital
Crew Road
Edinburgh
Tel: 031-332 2525

Canada
Sunnybrook Medical Center
2075 Bayview Avenue
Toronto
Ontario
M4N 3M5

Dr S.E.C. Turvey
1030 West Georgia Street
Vancouver
British Columbia
V6E 2Y6

Australia
Neurology Clinic
Flinders Medical Centre
South Road
Bedford Park
SA 5042

Headache and Pain Clinic
Queen Elizabeth Hospital
Woodville Road
Woodville
SA 5011

Pain Management Centre
520 Collins Street
Melbourne
VIC 3000

Neurology Clinic
Prince Henry Hospital
Anzac Parade
Little Bay
New South Wales 2036

Neurological Department
Royal North Shore Hospital
Pacific Highway
St Leonards
New South Wales 2065

Headache Clinic
Royal Brisbane Hospital
Herston Road
Herston
QLD 4006

New Zealand
Neurological Clinic
Auckland Hospital
Park Road
Grafton
Auckland

Clinical School of Medicine
Christchurch Hospital
Riccarton Avenue
Christchurch

Wellington Clinical School
Wellington Hospital
Riddiford Street
Wellington

RECOMMENDED READING

The following books have been written by medically qualified doctors. Some are neurologists, but all have years of experience dealing with patients suffering with migraine and other types of headache.

The Headache and Migraine Book
Dr J.N. Blau
Corgi Books

Migraine
Dr Edda Hanington
Priory Press

Headache
Professor J.W. Lance
Charles Scribner's Sons, New York

Migraine, The Evolution of a Common Disorder
Dr Oliver W. Sacks
Duckworth (Paperback edition: Pan Books)

More Than Two Aspirin
Dr Seymour Diamond and W.B. Furlong
Follett

Living with Migraine
Dr Marcia Wilkinson
Heineman Health Booklet

A detailed reference book on alternative medicine is:
The Handbook of Complementary Medicine
Stephen Fulder
Coronet

ABOUT THE AUTHORS

F. CLIFFORD ROSE, FRCP is Physician-in-Charge at the Princess Margaret Migraine Clinic, Charing Cross Hospital, London, the leading hospital migraine clinic in the United Kingdom.

He has written six books and many magazine articles on migraine, and lectures and broadcasts regularly on the subject throughout the world.

PAUL DAVIES, MRCP is Registrar at the Princess Margaret Migraine Clinic. He is also a leading authority on migraine and has written and lectured widely on the subject.